Knowing Christ

Knowing Christ

believing

Edited by
Ray E. Barnwell, Sr.

WESLEYAN
PUBLISHING HOUSE

Indianapolis, Indiana

Contributing Writers and Editors

Ray E. Barnwell, Sr.
James Blackburn
Martha Blackburn
Karl Eastlack
Mari Gonlag
Steven Lennox
Darlene Teague
Earle L. Wilson
H. C. Wilson
Lawrence W. Wilson
Mark O. Wilson
Norman G. Wilson

Discipleship Project Committee

Earle L. Wilson, Chairman
Ray Barnwell, Sr., Project Director
Martha Blackburn
Dan Berry
Donald D. Cady
Ross DeMerchant
Steve DeNeff
James Dunn
Russ Gunsalus
Ron McClung
Robert Brown, Advisory Member
Darlene Teague, Advisory Member

Table of Contents

Preface

Everything has a beginning: the world, each day, every person, even your faith in Christ. When you became a believer in Christ, your life had a new beginning. As Jesus said, you were "born again." Let me be one of the first to welcome you to the family of God. I am excited about your decision to follow Jesus.

As part of God's family, you are His child and He is your Father. And just as every good earthly father wants to see his children grow, your Heavenly Father wants to see you mature also. Your growth and development are foremost in His mind. He wants you to become more and more like Him.

You may be thinking, "Me? Be like God? That's not possible!"

Yes, it is possible. You can grow to become the godly person that He wants you to be. Of course, that won't happen overnight. Your development involves more than a single moment of decision or one week's church attendance. It's a process, a lifelong journey. That journey is called *discipleship.*

But let's get back to you. Your journey began with your decision to follow Christ, and it has led you to this book, *Knowing Christ: believing*, a part of the *Building Faith* series. This unique series of books is designed to help you grow in the faith. It has been written with you in mind. We are honored that we can join you on this journey.

Important spiritual guides on your journey will include your pastor, Sunday School teacher or small group leader, Christian relatives and friends, and perhaps a mentor or an accountability partner. You may be asking why you would need all these people on your journey. Remember that Satan, the enemy of your soul, uses a variety of weapons to dampen your faith. Right now, your faith is strong, like a hot fire. Satan will try to drown it out. One way of doing that is to isolate you from other believers. When you remove a single log from a fire, it soon goes out. But when several logs burn together, they fuel one another. In the same way, you need other Christians in order to keep your faith burning brightly.

This book may also feed your faith in Christ. I hope you'll read it carefully. And be sure to read the introduction. It will help you make the most of this book. Think of it as a backpack filled with the supplies you'll need for a day's hike.

Here's a snapshot of what's ahead in *Knowing Christ: believing.*

Chapter one is about spiritual formation. It will show you how to grow as a new believer. It provides an overview of the journey and some of the equipment you will need to make it all the way.

The second chapter will help you understand what happened when you made your personal decision to follow Christ. It will also help you respond to others when they ask, "What's different about you?"

Chapter three is focused on the importance of the Bible in your new life. You will learn how to choose a version of the Bible, how to study it, and how to apply biblical principles to your life.

You'll discover the importance of sharing your newfound faith in Christ in chapter four. You will learn why it's so important to tell this story and how to go about it.

The fifth chapter explores the deeper life that's possible for every Christian. You will learn what it means to be holy and how you can be holy too.

Many people first learn about God through a worship service. In chapter six you will explore the meaning and practice of Christian worship.

Your life is a gift from God, and chapter seven shows the importance of managing that sacred trust wisely. You'll discover how to live a life that shows respect for God in the use of your time, abilities, and resources.

The concluding chapter shows the importance of having healthy Christian relationships.

Once again, welcome! I'm glad you're along on the journey of *Building Faith.*

RAY E. BARNWELL, SR.

Introduction

Welcome to the exciting journey of discipleship! This book—part of the *Building Faith* series—offers a great opportunity for spiritual growth. In fact, the entire series has been developed for just that purpose: to help you grow as a disciple of Jesus Christ. By participating in this study, you will be shaping your life according to God's Word by using spiritual disciplines such as Bible study, prayer, fasting, Scripture memorization, meditation, and journal writing.

The Goal: Building People

Discipleship is the continuing process of spiritual development. It begins at conversion and continues as long as we live—it's a lifelong journey. Our strategy for making disciples is called *Building People*. The *Building People Strategy* is built upon four core values:

- Sharing Love—Evangelism
- Shaping Lives—Discipleship
- Serving Like Christ—Ministering to Society
- Sending Leaders—Mobilization

Here's how it works: having discovered Christ, you will want to grow in your knowledge of Him—shaping your life according to God's Word. As you do, you will discover a personal ministry, a way to use your spiritual gifts to serve others. Then, having been filled with compassion for others, you will be moved to go into the world, fulfilling the Great Commission by evangelizing the lost—thus completing the cycle of discipleship.

The Process: Building Faith

We implement the *Building People Strategy* through a process called *Building Faith. Building Faith* is a *competencies model*, meaning that it's focused on integrating important abilities into every aspect of a believer's life. These core competencies are organized around five categories:

- Biblical Beliefs
- Lifestyle Practices
- Virtues
- Core Values
- Mission

This process aims to form disciples according to the *Great Commandment* and the *Great Commission.*

The method is summarized in the chart that follows. You'll want to bookmark this page and refer to it often.

Building Faith

Foundational Beliefs	Lifestyle Practices	Personal Virtues	Core Values	Mission
The Trinity	Worship	Joy	Biblical Authority	Discipling Believers
Salvation by Grace	Prayer and Faith	Peace and Grace	Biblical Authority	Evangelizing the Lost
Authority of the Bible	Practicing the Mind of Christ and Discipline	Faithfulness	Biblical Authority	Discipling Believers; Equipping the Church
Personal Relationship with God	Bible Study and Prayer	Self-Control	Christlikeness; Disciple-Making	Discipling Believers
Identity in Christ	Baptism, Lord's Supper	Humility and Grace	Local Church Centered	Discipling Believers
Church/ Family of God	Biblical Community of Faith Beginning in a Christian Home	Love	Local Church Centered; Servant Leadership	Ministering to Society; Discipling Believers
Eternity/Global Evangelism	Lifestyle Evangelism	Love and Obedience	Disciple-Making; Unity in Diversity	Evangelizing the Lost
Stewardship (Including Good Works, Compassion)	Making Christ Lord of Time, Money, Life	Humility, Patience and Goodness	Disciple-Making; Servant Leadership	Equipping the Church; Ministering to Society
Freedom of the Will	Biblical World View	Obedience	Cultural Relevance; Biblical Authority	Discipling Believers; Equipping the Church
Holiness	Godliness, Loving Obedience to God's Revealed Will	Patience, Gentleness, Kindness, Love	Christlikeness; Disciple-Making	Discipling Believers; Ministering to Society

Foundational Truths

Building Faith is based on ten foundational truths, which are key elements for life transformation. These biblical concepts encompass the scope of Christian thinking. Learning these important concepts will help you grow in the faith.

Practices

Every believer must move from theory to practice. That is, he or she must learn to apply biblical truth to life. The practices identified in *Building Faith* will assist you to enact your faith and will become the evidence of the change that's taken place in your life.

Virtues

Virtues are Christlike qualities that emerge in the life of a believer, replacing sinful thoughts and attitudes. These virtues reveal the developing character of a transformed person and attract others to Christ. These virtues are also known as the *fruit of the Spirit.*

Core Values

Biblical truth must be applied in the framework of Christ's body, the church. The core values are the guiding principles by which the church should function. They are our method of operating, describing *how* we do the things we do.

Mission

Ultimately, believers are called to serve. The mission describes what it is that we do for Christ. Each biblical truth finds a practical expression in our work.

Your Involvement: Spiritual Disciplines

These days, many people who are searching for faith have discovered something exciting in Christian worship. The worship service is the point of entry to most churches. Yet as important as worship is, believers need something more in order to grow in the faith. Most of the new believers I speak with still have questions; they're looking for clarification. And they are longing for Christian relationships. Wouldn't it be great if there was a place you could go to make friends and find answers? Wouldn't it be wonderful if you could discover a forum to open your heart, grow in the faith, and find unconditional love?

There is such a place!

Sunday School and other small group discipleship settings provide exactly that kind of environment for building faith. Discipleship moves beyond worship to involve people in building their faith in the context of loving relationships. Just as the New Testament church was built on teaching and preaching (Acts 5:42), so today's church must be built on Bible study. Gaining a thorough knowledge of the Bible is best done by participating in a Sunday School class or Bible study group in addition to attending worship services. Both are important. One without the other can create an imbalance in your spiritual life. Being connected to a family-like unit that's relationship based is a vital component of discipleship.

In most churches, that caring, nurturing unit is called Sunday School. Other churches achieve this interaction through discipleship groups of various kinds. Whatever the name, day, or place of meeting, the fact is that everyone needs a protected environment in which to discover and practice the faith.

If you want to grow and become more effective in the Christian faith, then I urge you to join a Sunday School class or discipleship group.

Along with involvement in a discipleship class or small group, there are some other simple disciplines that have been proven to enhance spiritual formation. You can boost your spiritual growth by using these simple tools.

Bible Reading and Study

The *Building Faith* series is designed to direct you to the Bible at every point in your study. Each chapter begins with one or two important Scripture passages and includes dozens of Bible references to explore. You can enhance your Bible study by using a good Bible translation, written in today's language, such as the New International Version (NIV).

Scripture Memorization

Memorization is a simple way to gain ownership of important Scripture verses. Each of the chapters in this book includes a key verse to memorize. At the end of the book is a Scripture memory tool—perforated flash cards containing the key verse for each chapter. Use them to memorize these verses and you'll gain confidence in your knowledge of Scripture.

Daily Prayer and Reflection

Time alone with God is perhaps the single most important spiritual practice for any disciple. Spend time in prayer and reflection every day.

A Personal Spiritual Journal

Journal writing is a way to enhance time spent in prayer and reflection. Recording observations about your life and faith will help you process what you are learning and clarify the spiritual issues in your life. There is a personal spiritual journal page included in each chapter of this book. At the end of each book is an extended journal section that you may use to expand your journal writing. Take this study as your opportunity to begin the practice of journal writing. You'll be glad you did.

Now, let's get started on the exciting journey of *Building Faith!*

CHAPTER 1

Growing in Your New Life

Spiritual Formation

Do not conform any longer to the pattern of this world, but be transformed by the renewing of your mind. Then you will be able to test and approve what God's will is—his good, pleasing and perfect will.

—Romans 12:2

 **Bible Basics**

Galatians 4:19

¹⁹My dear children, for whom I am again in the pains of childbirth until Christ is formed in you. . . .

Ephesians 4:14–15

¹⁴Then we will no longer be infants, tossed back and forth by the waves, and blown here and there by every wind of teaching. . . . ¹⁵Instead, speaking the truth in love, we will in all things grow up into him who is the Head, that is, Christ.

🐲 Connecting God's Word to Life

Circle the key words in these passages. What does it mean to have Christ formed in you? How do you think this process takes place?

The Importance of Being Pliable

As a young child, I had a fascination with Play-Doh. It was such fun to mold and shape the brightly colored dough, one minute forming a dog and the next minute a bird or a flower. The possibilities were endless, and the joy was as much in the process as the product. Squeeze, shape, cut a little here, and add a little there—perhaps the best part was that failures could be erased with one stroke as a misshapen object was reformed. As long as the dough was moist and soft, great creations were possible.

Spiritual growth is much more serious than playing with Play-Doh, yet there are some parallels. Personal growth is a process that involves molding and shaping, cutting and adding, with pressure applied in just the right places to reshape us into Christ's likeness. In this process, the "dough" must remain pliable in the hands of the Master Craftsman, our Heavenly Father, if He is to make our lives into the perfect treasures that bear His image.

The Bible frequently talks about this process—which we call *spiritual formation*—whereby our lives are progressively changed to be more like Christ. In Rom. 12:2, the Apostle Paul urges us not to be conformed (similar, identical, or obedient) to the pattern of the world (the things our culture accepts and expects). Rather, we are to be transformed (changed in structure, appearance, character, or condition) by the renewing of our minds. In 2 Cor. 3:18 he says that believers "are being transformed into his likeness," becoming more and more like Christ. The descriptive phrase from Gal. 4:19, "until Christ is formed in you," assures us that God intends to change us so completely that Christ Himself will live within us, directing every aspect of our lives. In fact, a Christian's inner being is transformed so radically that that person becomes a "new creation" (2 Cor. 5:17).

And what is the goal of this process? That we might become mature, complete, and holy people (Col. 1:28–29). God will be content with nothing less than our complete transformation. And God Himself is the One who makes this change a reality.

How do you respond to the idea that God wants to reshape your life? Are you willing or resistant? Why?

Our Sources of Truth

Just how does God go about the work of transforming us into the image of Christ? And what is our role in the process?

John Wesley, the eighteenth-century evangelist whose life, ministry, and writings have shaped many believers, taught that there are four primary sources of truth. These are Scripture, reason, tradition, and experience.

The foundation of our faith is Scripture—the Bible. Because Wesley believed that God Himself had inspired and guided the process of writing and compiling the Bible, he was convinced that its teachings provide the basis for all that we believe about God. Through meditation and study of the Bible, God begins His work of transformation in our lives.

While the Bible provides our foundation for truth, God has created us as rational beings. He has given us the ability to think (Isa. 1:18) and He expects us to use it. Christianity is neither unreasonable nor irrational. Therefore, reason informs our understanding of Scripture.

God has also given us the church. The traditions of the church—those beliefs and practices that have been handed down from the time of Christ to the present day—are also important for understanding the truth. We can learn a great deal from faithful people who have gone before us. While not equal to Scripture, tradition is an important source of truth. Christians think seriously about their faith and struggle with the hard questions of life and belief according to God's plan.

Finally, Wesley believed that our own experience of God's work in our lives is an important teacher. Through the Holy Spirit, God communicates with us in understandable ways.

Wesley's sources of truth are also called the Wesley Quadrilateral. It can be pictured as a stool, with Scripture at the top, supported by tradition, experience, and reason.

These are the tools that God uses to communicate truth to us, and they are consistent; if we truly understand what God is teaching us through each source, their messages agree. God doesn't give mixed messages!

List some things you have learned from each of these four sources of truth.

Think

Scripture:

Reason:

Tradition:

Experience:

Getting to Know God

God's plan for our discipleship is truly multifaceted. He reveals Himself to us in a number of ways that we can know Him personally and intimately. Yet that process must begin somewhere. Now that you have come to believe in God, how do you go about developing a relationship with Him?

There are several spiritual disciplines that Christians have used for centuries to aid them in getting to know God.

Spending Time Alone with God

In human relationships, we generally move from one level of relationship to a deeper one by spending time together. People who are acquaintances become friends after socializing, talking, and being together. It's hard to build a quality friendship with someone you see only in a crowd.

In the same way, getting to know God involves spending time with Him. Our relationship with Him grows as we invest time in just being with Him and listening as He speaks through His Word and through the Holy Spirit.

> God will seldom scream to get our attention. If we're going to get to know God, we'll need to make time for Him.

In today's culture we rarely take time to just be quiet. But God will seldom scream to get our attention. If we're going to get to know God, we'll need to make time for Him.

Establish a Regular Time

The challenge of finding time to set apart for God seems overwhelming because our lives are so busy. But think about the human relationships that are important to you. Somehow you make the time to spend with those you love. When we offer even a few minutes to God each day, it is our gift of love in response to His love for us. Establish a regular time every day to spend with God. For some people it works best in the morning when they are fresh. This way it sets the tone for the day. For other people, an evening time works better. Do whatever works best for you.

Find a Special Place

Going to the same place at the same time every day makes it easier to establish the habit of meeting with God. If you have a family, they will also get to know your routine and when they should leave you alone.

Be Spontaneous

Because you have a daily appointment with God doesn't mean that you can't meet Him at other times. Use enough routine to establish the habit of spending time with God but enough spontaneity to make the time enjoyable.

Start Small

Don't begin by trying to spend an hour with God each day. If you are trying to build a good habit, you can kill it at the start by having an unrealistic goal. Begin with a shorter time, like five or ten minutes, and let it expand as you discover more ways to communicate with Him. As you begin to meet with God regularly, you will find that your desire to spend time with Him grows.

Use a Guide

It may be helpful, especially in the beginning, to have a source of input for your time with God. There are lots of good devotional tools available today, with one to fit every interest and personality. A guide that includes a daily Bible reading, a devotional meditation, and perhaps suggestions for prayer may be helpful.

Using these hints, what will you do this week to make a daily time with God a reality in your life?

Knowing God's Word

Did you ever get a postcard from a friend who wanted to share a new experience with you? Perhaps you've received a love letter at some time. Or maybe you've received an E-mail from someone you respected, giving advice about a problem.

God's Word, the Bible, is all of these things. It is His written communication to us. Sometimes it reads like a love letter, sometimes like a historical document, and sometimes like a great novel. But throughout its pages it reveals the God who is unseen yet appears in every aspect of history and throughout every day of our lives.

Since the Bible is God's written revelation, it is the most clear and objective source of information about Him. The Bible shows us who God is, what He is doing in the world, and how to know Him better. And the Bible is reliable. God will never tell us to do something that is not supported in His written Word. It keeps us on the right track in following Christ.

Here are some ways that you can get to know God better through His Word.

Read the Bible

The Bible should have a prominent place in your daily time with God. Daily Bible reading will give you His truth a little bit at a time. Your readings may accompany a devotional guide or may be more systematic, such as the reading of a particular book of the Bible in its entirety. Each of these methods is good and should probably be used at one time or another.

> Daily Bible reading will give you His truth a little bit at a time. Gaining knowledge of God's Word is a first step.

If you are looking for a place to start, try the Gospel of Mark or John. In these portraits of Jesus you will begin to see what God is like, for in Jesus, God's Word became a human being!

If you are unfamiliar with the Bible, you will likely find the New Testament a bit easier to read than the Old Testament. That doesn't mean you should skip the Old Testament! There is great wisdom there that every Christian needs. But you may want to start with the Gospels (Matthew, Mark, Luke, and John), and then move to some of the New Testament letters (sometimes called Epistles) such as 1 and 2 Corinthians or Ephesians.

Along the way, begin weaving some Psalms and Proverbs from the Old Testament into your reading, then move to the book of Genesis. It reads like an ancient novel, telling the stories of the patriarchs like Abraham, Isaac, and Jacob. Eventually, you will become comfortable reading from both Testaments, and God will become real to you as you read His book!

Meditate on God's Word

One songwriter poured out his heart to God in Ps. 119:97: "Oh, how I love your law! I meditate on it all day long." As you read the Bible, you will learn more about who God is and what He has said. Gaining knowledge of God's Word is a first step.

But knowing the facts only takes you so far. Your goal is to know God, not just what He has said. One way of doing that is to meditate on portions of the Bible.

Meditation is contemplation and reflection on a portion of Scripture. For example, you might choose to meditate on John the Baptist's statement about Jesus in John 3:30: "He must become greater; I must become less." You might reflect on what John meant by that and on what it may mean in your life to "become less." In this case, you might ponder a series of questions before God, such as:

- What prompted John to make this statement? How is my situation like John's?

- How can Jesus become greater in my life?

- What does it mean to become less? How might I become less?

- What needs to change in my life for Jesus to become greater and for me to become less?

- Am I willing to allow God to change me in this way?

Meditation helps you apply Scripture to your life. When you meditate, the Bible is no longer an abstract rulebook, but a living tool that God can use to transform your life.

Study the Bible

When you think of Bible study, you probably think of a small group activity led by someone who is very knowledgeable about the Bible. Group Bible study is a great setting for spiritual growth, but personal Bible study is also important for your spiritual formation.

> There are riches to be discovered in God's Word, but it will take some effort on your part to discover them.

Bible reading is a great start, but sooner or later you'll want to dig deeper, learning all you can from God's Word. To do that, you may choose to study a particular book of the Bible for an extended time, reading from the book regularly and using study aids to analyze what you read.

Some study aids that you might use are a study Bible that includes introductory notes about each book, commentaries that offer detailed explanations of each verse, or Bible dictionaries that list background information on the people, places, and events in the Bible.

There are riches to be discovered in God's Word, but it will take some effort on your part to discover them. Consider purchasing some general Bible study tools such as those listed in the *To Learn More* section of this chapter.

The Apostle Paul wrote, "Do your best to present yourself to God as one approved, a workman who does not need to be ashamed and who correctly handles the word of truth" (2 Tim. 2:15). Study God's Word so that you will know it thoroughly.

Memorize Bible Verses

"I have hidden your word in my heart that I might not sin against you, O LORD" (Ps. 119:11). That well-known psalm points to another tool that forms us into the people God wants us to be. That is Bible memorization.

Many of us were required to memorize bits of poetry or literature in school. The practice of memorization became distasteful, partly because the content seemed meaningless. That line from Shakespeare may have been eloquent poetry, but it's hard to see how it related to daily life.

But God's Word is living and active. For those who possess it, it is a shield in times of temptation and a ray of hope in times of crisis.

For instance, you may be facing a challenging time in your life. You are discouraged, tempted to despair. Then you recall the words of Jesus from Matt. 28:20, "And surely I am with you always, to the very end of the age." As you recall the promise of Christ, you gain courage to face the days ahead.

Or perhaps you received bad news from the doctor and fear threatens to overwhelm you. But a memory verse from Isa. 12:2 helps you hang on: "Surely God is my salvation; I will trust and not be afraid. . . ." God gives you peace because your hope is in Him.

Memorizing God's Word is always worthwhile and can provide just the wisdom you need to face life's challenges. Make Bible memorization a regular part of your spiritual formation. There are Scripture memory cards located in the back of this book to aid you in developing this practice.

Describe the role that Scripture plays in your life. List two or three things you will do to know God better through His Word.

Communicating with God

Prayer is communication with God. As such, it may serve several needs. In prayer, unbelievers cry out to God for forgiveness and mercy. In prayer, believers worship, adore, and give thanks to God. In prayer, we ask for God's help to face the challenges of life. When we pray, we come to God in complete dependence, offering our weakness to God's strength, our failure to God's perfection, our inadequacies to God's power. By communicating with Him, we come to know Him more fully and to accept His will. We are further transformed into His image.

Talk to God. Some people think of prayer as a mysterious activity or as a very formal sort of speech, filled with "thee's" and "thou's." In reality, prayer is just talking to God. And God understands your language! Talk to Him as you would to a friend. Imagine that God is there with you in conversation—He is! Share with Him your sorrows and hurts, your deep desires and needs, and your greatest joys. God urges us to communicate with Him, and He promises that He will hear and respond (Jer. 29:12).

Confess Sin

As you talk with God, remember that you are keeping very distinguished company. You are in the presence of the King of Kings and Lord of Lords. As you recognize that you are in the presence of a perfect, holy, all-powerful God, you are likely to see things about your life that fall far short of His standards. Whether those things are willful acts of disobedience or unintentional shortcomings in your attempts to live according to God's standards, confess them to God (Ps. 38:18–22). Ask for the wisdom to know how to live for Him and the will to do what is right. Admit that you are dependent on the One who is "able to keep you from falling and to present you before his glorious presence without fault and with great joy." (Jude 1:24).

> In reality, prayer is just talking to God. And God understands your language!

Ask for Help

Jesus promised that if we ask, He will answer; if we seek Him, we will find Him; and if we knock, the door will be opened to us (Matt. 7:7). When you pray, ask for God's help and guidance, both for yourself and for others.

This kind of prayer is known as *intercessory prayer.* The Bible tells us that Jesus intercedes for us (Rom. 8:34). He also showed us how to intercede when He prayed in John 17 for His disciples, other believers, and those who would eventually believe. The Apostle Paul, too, often demonstrated intercession in his prayer for others (see Eph. 1:8; 2 Cor. 13:7; Col. 1:3).

> Remember to pray for spiritual—not just physical or material—needs for yourself and others.

But what kinds of things should we ask God for? The Bible tells us that we can present requests about anything before God (Eph. 6:18; Phil. 4:6). He cares about all of our needs. Yet Jesus showed us in the Lord's Prayer (see Matt. 6:9–13) that God is especially concerned about spiritual needs. Here are some of the people and things we are told to pray for in the New Testament.

- The establishment of God's kingdom and the enactment of His will (Matt. 6:10)
- Provision for our daily needs (Matt. 6:11)
- Christian workers for evangelistic ministry (Luke 10:2)
- Spiritual leaders (Col. 4:3)
- Open doors for ministry to other people (Rom. 1:10)
- Government leaders and others in authority (1 Tim. 2:2)
- Our enemies (Luke 6:28)
- Wisdom (James 1:5)
- Spiritual enlightenment (Eph. 1:18)
- Spiritual strength (Eph. 3:17)

When he gave instructions on prayer, the Apostle James demonstrated the need for balance between earthly and spiritual concerns (see James 5:13–20). It is easy for our prayers to get "earthbound." Remember to pray for spiritual—not just physical or material—needs for yourself and others.

Say "Thank You"

Our prayers should include praise and thanks for who God is and for the things He is doing in our lives. As David said, "I will give thanks to the LORD because of his righteousness and will sing praise to the name of the LORD Most High" (Ps. 7:17). Throughout the Old Testament, the people of Israel were quick to praise and thank God for His goodness, His gifts, His grace, His mercy, and all of the other blessings He provided (see 1 Kings 8:56). Not only does our praise and thanksgiving acknowledge and honor God, it proclaims His goodness to others (Ps. 9:11), silences God's enemies (Ps. 8:2), and lifts our own spirits as we remember His love for us.

Listen to God

God not only listens when we pray, He responds! Through the prophet Jeremiah, God said, "Call to me and I will answer you and tell you great and unsearchable things you do not know" (Jer. 33:3). Like a parent who gives good things to his children, God wants to respond to us with good gifts, all of the things that are best for us (Matt. 7:9–11). In the Gospels we are promised that our loving Father hears our requests and responds to them (John 16:23–27).

> When you pray, listen for the "voice" of God. Just as you learn to recognize a human voice, you will learn to recognize God's voice.

When you pray, listen for the "voice" of God. As you pray, you may come to see the solution to a problem you've struggled with, or understand a situation that has troubled you, or accept some truth that you have resisted. These quiet moments of realization are times when God "speaks" to you through His Holy Spirit. God does not speak with an audible voice, but communicates with you nonetheless. Just as you learn to recognize a human voice, you will learn to recognize God's voice. It just takes regular practice!

Prayer is not some magic formula uttered to make God give us what we want. Rather, it is one aspect of our communication with God, communication that nurtures our growing relationship with God. And building a healthy relationship requires listening as well as talking.

Pray in Faith

God promises to respond to our prayers, but asks that we pray in faith (see Matt. 9:29; 17:20). Here are some biblical instructions for praying with a faithful heart. We are to:

- Ask with faith, believing God will answer (Mark 11:24);
- Ask with a forgiven and forgiving heart (Mark 11:25);
- Ask with the right motives—for God's pleasure, not ours (James 4:3);
- Ask from the basis of an obedient life (1 John 3:22);
- Ask for things in accordance with God's will (1 John 5:14).

When you pray, examine your heart. Listen as God speaks to you about your own motives and desires. No, we will not always get everything we want from God. As with young and immature children begging their parents for things they want, we sometimes ask God for things that would not be good for us. Sometimes God, in His love, has to protect us from our own desires. But when we pray in faith, living obediently and seeking His will, we can have confidence that He will hear and respond.

Rely on the Holy Spirit

At times, prayer is difficult because it is so subjective and intangible. You can't physically see or hear the One with whom you are conversing, so how do you know there's anyone there? The disciples faced this same problem when Jesus revealed that He would leave the earth. They were afraid they would lose their intimate relationship with God (see John 13). Jesus countered their fear with one of His greatest promises—the promise to send the Holy Spirit.

The Holy Spirit, Jesus said, would not only be with us, but also in us (John 14:17). And it is the Holy Spirit's job to teach us what we need to know (John 14:26), to remind us of Jesus' teaching (John 14:27), to make us conscious of sin (John 16:8–9), and to help us find our way into the future (John 16:13). The Spirit even helps us pray (Rom. 8:26).

When you pray, be sensitive to the Spirit. Sometimes He will remind us of Jesus' teachings or of our own sinful behavior. At other times He will bring peace to our confusion and frustration. Occasionally He will prompt us to act in a particular way. However He "speaks" to you, learn to recognize His voice and respond with obedience to His direction. Just as in a human relationship, the better you know God the easier it is to know and share and follow His desires and guidance in your life.

> When you pray, be sensitive to the Spirit. However He "speaks" to you, learn to recognize His voice and respond with obedience to His direction.

Using Other Spiritual Disciplines

Spending time with God, learning His Word, and praying are three important spiritual practices or *disciplines*. There are a number of other spiritual disciplines that Christians use to further their spiritual formation. Here are a few.

Keep a Journal

As you read and study the Bible and pray regularly, you may benefit from writing down your ideas, insights, and prayers. This discipline may help you in several ways. You will have a concrete reminder of the things you have learned, the commitments you have made, and the prayers you've prayed. You will also have a source of encouragement. Reviewing what you've written in months or years past will remind you of the ways God has answered prayer and helped you to grow. There is space for journal writing included in this book. Why not use it to begin recording your spiritual journey?

Find a Mentor

Sometimes it's helpful to have a friend who can give advice or support. Identify a mature Christian who can serve as a mentor to you. You might associate with this person informally, observing his or her life and faith, asking occasional questions. Or you might formalize the relationship, meeting regularly to discuss the Scriptures, the faith, and your spiritual growth.

Fast

Fasting—abstaining from food for a period of time—is one of the oldest spiritual disciplines. Jesus fasted in the wilderness (Luke 4:2), and the early Christians fasted also (see Acts 13:2; 14:23). Going without a meal provides time for concentrated prayer, and the experience of hunger focuses the mind on God. Consider fasting occasionally as an aid to your spiritual formation.

How well do you listen to God? What things might you do to become a better listener?

Changing and Being Changed

Change is a fact of life. All living things are constantly changing—either developing or decaying. Generally, when something is growing, it becomes larger—greater.

That's not necessarily the case in your spiritual life.

At one point during His ministry, Jesus' disciples asked Him who was the greatest person in the kingdom of heaven. His answer must have startled them, for He said that all of them must "change and become like little children" (Matt. 18:3).

> Spiritual formation is all about our willingness to be transformed into the likeness of Christ.

It seems contradictory. We could understand an instruction to become like adults. But to become like children? How does it fit with the Apostle Peter's command to "grow up into your salvation" (1 Pet. 2:2)?

Jesus used the image of a child to convey the importance of humility, simplicity, innocence, and dependence in our relationship with God. Spiritual formation is all about our willingness to be transformed into the likeness of Christ. We must not be resistant, but yielded; not experts, but learners; not talkers, but listeners. As we become childlike in our dependence on Him, He can form us into all He wants us to be, something more than we ever dreamed possible! (Eph. 3:20).

To Learn More

How to Read the Bible for All It's Worth by Gordon Fee and Douglas Stuart

Devotional Life in the Wesleyan Tradition by Steven Harper

Ministry Dynamics for a New Century: The Dynamics of Spiritual Formation by Mel Lawrenz

Shaped by the Word: The Power of Scripture in Spiritual Formation by Robert M. Mulholland

Hearing God: Developing a Conversational Relationship with God by Dallas Willard

All additional books and resources are available from Wesleyan Publishing House at www.wesleyan.org/wph or by calling 800.4.WESLEY.

Personal Spiritual Journal

DATE _____

_____

_____

_____

_____

_____

_____

_____

_____

_____

_____

_____

_____

_____

My Prayer Today—

_____

_____

_____

_____

CHAPTER 2

Understanding What God Did for You

Salvation

Salvation is found in no one else, for there is no other name under heaven given to men by which we must be saved.

—Acts 4:12

 **Bible Basics**

Acts 16:29–31

²⁹The jailer called for lights, rushed in, and fell trembling before Paul and Silas. ³⁰He then brought them out and asked, "Sirs, what must I do to be saved?" ³¹They replied, "Believe in the Lord Jesus, and you will be saved—you and your household."

John 3:3

"I tell you the truth, unless a man is born again, he cannot see the kingdom of God."

John 3:16

For God so loved the world that He gave His one and only Son, that whoever believes in Him shall not perish but have eternal life.

Romans 5:1–2

> [1]Therefore, since we have been justified through faith, we have peace with God through our Lord Jesus Christ, [2]through whom we have gained access into this grace in which we now stand. And we rejoice in the hope of the glory of God.

Titus 3:5

> He saved us, not because of righteous things we had done, but because of His mercy. He saved us through the washing of rebirth and renewal by the Holy Spirit.

 Connecting God's Word to Life

Reflect on your experience of coming to know Christ as your personal Savior. Write a brief account of your own salvation.

Our Need for Salvation

The Bible is a book of salvation. While it speaks of many things, including prophets and kings, laws and covenants, miracles and mysteries, it is not primarily a book of history. It is really about how, by God's grace, we may be saved.

But who needs to be saved? Do *we* need to be saved? Why?

The Bible declares in 1 Cor. 15:3 that "Christ died for our sins in accordance with the scriptures." The fact that Christ died is a historical reality that can easily be verified. When we say, however, that Christ died *for our sins*, we're speaking of something more than a historical fact. If Christ died *for us*, then His death becomes personal; it has implications for every individual. Christ's death on the cross was not merely a human tragedy; it was an act of deliverance! We were in need of help, and God sent His Son to our rescue.

But we've gotten ahead of ourselves. If Christ died for us, there must be a reason. And to discover that reason, we must travel all the way back to the beginning.

The Problem of Sin

When God created Adam and Eve, the first two people in the world, He was pleased with His creation. It was pure and good. But Satan entered the scene and tempted our first parents to eat of the tree of the knowledge of good and evil, which was forbidden by God. Satan convinced them that when they ate of the fruit of that particular tree, they would be like God. So they ate; they sinned. They fell from God's favor and were expelled from the Garden of Eden.

As you think about your own life, isn't it true that there has been a tug-of-war going on within you? At times you want to do what is right and at other times you want what you know is wrong. Perhaps at times you wanted to be obedient to your parents or others in authority over you, even God, but at other times you wanted to break free and do your own thing.

In what ways did you rebel against God before you became a Christian?

The Effect of the Fall

Adam and Eve tried to live their lives without God. Having been made in the image of God, they lost some, though not all, of that Divine image. Since we are the offspring of Adam and Eve, we lost a great deal when they fell. None of us is what we ought to be, what we were meant to be. Apart from Christ, we live in rebellion against God; we live more for self than for God and others. At times we want to be good, but often we are not. This is what the Bible says about it, "There is none righteous, not even one" (Rom. 3:10).

The Bible also says in 1 Cor. 15:22, "In Adam all die." All people are born in sin. Sin is not just an action. It is also a state of being. We are born into a sinful condition, and our sinful acts are an expression of that. The image of God within us was damaged. In other words, we are both good and bad. We do have some good thoughts and good desires. At times we want to be good. But we are separated from God by our sinful condition, trapped in a life of habitual disobedience.

We all need salvation. We need to come back to God. We need God to forgive us and make things right with Him.

Look at the world. It's obvious that something is wrong. Races hate each other; husbands and wives turn against one another; people are addicted to alcohol and drugs; people rape and murder one another.

What's wrong with the world?

The simple answer is sin. Something must be done to deal with sin.

What evidence of sin do you see in your community? Your workplace? Your self?

Our Desire for Salvation

Everyone wants salvation. All people in every land on this planet reach out for a rescue from the condition of sin. Though they might not call it by that name, all people recognize that there is a problem in the world and in themselves. Every person longs to be someone he or she is not. Some would call this a quest for freedom. Others would describe it as a longing to be a better person. Still others would think of it as a desire to be safe—to be delivered from fear of death.

We see that longing for salvation in the pages of the Old Testament. There, the children of Israel thought of salvation as being safe or victorious as a nation. At the Exodus, deliverance from Egypt was a form of salvation by God. In fact, Moses said to the children of Israel: "Do not be afraid. Stand firm and you will see the deliverance the LORD will bring you today" (Exod. 14:13).

In the centuries before Christ, and even during the period of Christ's earthly ministry, people sought deliverance of some kind, but they despaired of seeing that salvation in their time. Life was difficult; there was much evil and hatred in the world. Rulers oppressed the people terribly, and many people lived in slavery so that while they longed for deliverance, they could not bring themselves to believe that it would come.

Later, when Christ came to earth, some of the Jews of His day did see Him as their deliverer. They believed He would save them from the domination of the Roman Empire. They later rejected Christ largely because He did not turn out to be a political deliverer. They were looking for national salvation; He offered personal, spiritual deliverance.

To this day, people are looking for a savior. Some look to politics, others to psychology or medicine or other sciences, some to economics. And some still refuse to believe that salvation is possible. But all are longing for a savior. But all are looking for a solution to the problem of sin.

In what ways did you look for salvation? What were you running away from? What were you running toward?

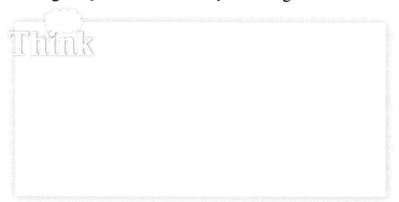

God's Plan for Us

The first few chapters of Genesis give the story of creation and the sad account of humankind's fall from fellowship with God. But the rest of the Bible tells about God's plan to restore that relationship. It's a wonderful story of the mighty acts of God, working to solve the problems caused by sin. It is the story of salvation.

That story begins in the Old Testament, where God began to work through people like Abraham, Moses, and the prophets. It continues in the New Testament, which records that God came to earth personally through His Son, Jesus Christ, to deliver us from sin.

Let's trace the steps that God took in making salvation available to each of us.

Preparation

The fall of humankind did not catch God off guard. He knew everything from the beginning. That does not mean, however, that God determined that Adam and Eve would sin. It simply means that even before they sinned, God knew about their actions and the result. And He had already created a plan to restore all people to Himself. The Bible says in Rev. 13:8 that Christ was the "Lamb slain from the foundation of the world." God anticipated that when given the choice, Adam and Eve would choose to sin. And He was prepared to offer His Son, the Lamb of God, to be the perfect sacrifice on our behalf.

> The fall of humankind did not catch God off guard. Even before they sinned, God knew about their actions and the result.

Incarnation: Christ's Birth

When Jesus was born in Bethlehem, as told in the wonderful Christmas story, what actually happened was that God became one of us. Christ Jesus was God, and He became a man "born of a woman, born under law" (Gal. 4:4).

This is a great mystery and wonderful miracle. Christ was fully God, without sin, the perfect One to die for our sins. At the same time, He was fully a human being. That baby in the manger really was the Son of God, and yet He was just like any other baby that was ever born. He cried, was hungry, needed His mother, and had wants and needs, just like you and me. He was 100 percent God and 100 percent human.

The Cross: Christ's Death

Jesus lived on earth for about thirty-three years. For three years, He traveled throughout ancient Palestine preaching the good news and performing great miracles. Finally, He was rejected by the authorities of His day and was put to death on the cross.

The Cross is central to our salvation because it provided the remedy for sin.

Although it was a cruel injustice in human terms, the Cross was part of God's plan to save the world. Paul wrote this about Christ's death in 2 Cor. 5:19, "God was reconciling the world to himself in Christ."

Because He was both God and man, Jesus could touch God with one hand and us with the other. When He died on the cross, His arms were outstretched. He reached to God and to us. And by dying for us, He made it possible for God and us to be brought together. This is called *the atonement*.

But did Christ have to die in order to accomplish this? If so, why?

According to God's plan, there can be no forgiveness for sin without bloodshed. In Lev. 17:11 we read: "For the life of a creature is in the blood, and I have given it to you to make atonement for yourselves on the altar; it is the blood that makes atonement for one's life." In Old Testament times, people received God's forgiveness through the slaughter of a lamb. The blood of the lamb symbolized life for the person offering the sacrifice.

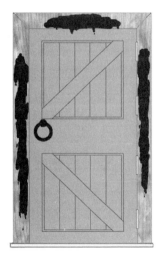

Also, during the Passover, when the children of Israel left Egypt, the blood of a lamb was splashed on the door posts and lintel of each home, symbolizing that a death had taken place. That symbolic act meant salvation for the ancient Israelites, and it looked forward to the day when Christ would die on the cross for us.

By His death—specifically, by the shedding of His blood—Christ provided salvation for all who believe in Him.

The Resurrection: Christ's New Life

The resurrection of Christ is all-important. Without the Resurrection we would have no reason to believe, no hope, no salvation. Why is the Resurrection so vital in the plan of salvation?

The Resurrection vindicates Jesus. The Jews thought He was a pretender, and at times His own disciples doubted Him. But the Resurrection proved that Christ really is God's Son. Peter preached on the day of Pentecost, "Let all Israel be assured of this: God has made this Jesus, whom you crucified, both Lord and Christ" (Acts 2:36).

Also, the Resurrection declares the triumph of God over the forces of sin and death. So the Apostle Paul can write with full confidence, "Death has been swallowed up in victory. Where, O death, is your victory? Where, O death, is your sting? The sting of death is sin, and the power of sin is the law. But thanks be to God! He gives us the victory through our Lord Jesus Christ" (1 Cor. 15:54–57).

The fact that Jesus was raised from the dead is what gives us hope for an eternal life. Because Jesus was raised, we know that we will be too.

The Ascension: Christ's Return to the Father

The ascension of Christ into heaven is recorded in Acts 1:9: "After he said this, he was taken up before their very eyes and a cloud hid him from their sight." The Ascension placed Christ at His rightful place—at the right hand of God the Father. This event relates to our salvation in three ways.

- *Exaltation:* Christ is exalted by the Father, lifted up all the way from the grave to the Father's right hand (Eph. 4:8–9).

- *Intercession:* Christ is at the Father's right hand right now, interceding on our behalf (Rom. 8:34; 1 John 2:1).

- *Comfort:* Jesus promised that after He was gone, the Comforter would come to us. His promise was fulfilled by the pouring out of the Holy Spirit upon Christ's followers (Acts 2:33; John 15:26; 16:7).

The Second Coming: Christ's Return

Christ's return is the final act in our salvation. The Bible says that "this same Jesus, who has been taken from you into heaven, will come back in the same way you have seen Him go into heaven" (Acts 1:11). We have already been delivered from the guilt, power, and penalty of sin through faith in Christ Jesus. But our redemption will not be complete until He returns and delivers us from the physical effects of sin.

> Our redemption will not be complete until He returns and delivers us from the physical effects of sin.

Salvation involves the salvation not only of individuals but also of the world. God has permitted Satan to exercise some power over human history, but God will not allow that to continue forever. God will one day take the reins of human governments in His hand, and His will shall be done on earth even as it is done in heaven. If it were not for Christ's final return, our redemption would be forever incomplete.

The Steps Christ Took to Save Us

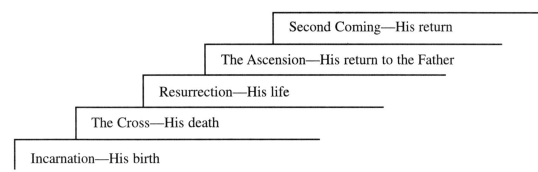

Second Coming—His return

The Ascension—His return to the Father

Resurrection—His life

The Cross—His death

Incarnation—His birth

What new ideas about God's plan for salvation have you learned from this chapter?

Receiving Christ Jesus as Savior

So we know why we need salvation—because of sin, which entered the world when Adam and Eve sinned in the Garden of Eden. Their sinful nature was passed on to us when we were born, keeping us from being in a right relationship with God. And we know what Christ did to provide salvation—He came to earth as a baby, died on the cross, arose from the dead, ascended into heaven, and plans to come again.

Since you are reading this book, it's likely that you have already realized your need for forgiveness and have reached out to God, accepting His gift of salvation.

Now the question! Exactly what happened when you were saved?

God's First Step: Grace

It's important to remember that salvation does not begin with us; it begins with God. Before you ever asked for God's forgiveness, you were drawn to Him by His Holy Spirit.

That action on God's part—that leading of the Holy Spirit that turns your heart toward God—is called *prevenient grace* (or *initial grace*). This grace precedes salvation. It prepares our hearts to meet God and enables us to respond when He offers forgiveness.

In Titus 2:11 we read: "For the grace of God that bring salvation has appeared to all men . . ." Grace is a gift. God, at the very beginning of the process of saving us offers us a gift. It is a gift of love. He loves you. He loves everybody.

You have had experiences of this initial grace of God. Think of the times you were moved by a song, an experience, a feeling of love or even sadness to feel sorry for your sins and to reach out to God. Perhaps there was a time when you said to yourself, "I should live a different life," or "I should start attending church," or "I should get my life in order." Thoughts like these are evidence of God's work in you. They were prompted by God's Holy Spirit so that you might open your heart to God and His will for you.

That's grace.

> It's important to remember that salvation does not begin with us; it begins with God.

Your First Step: Faith

Salvation depends entirely upon God making the first move toward you—prevenient grace. But God does not force salvation on anyone. Each of us has a free will. We may choose to believe in Him or we may choose not to believe.

If we are to be saved, we must believe.

Most people begin by believing historical things about God. For example, they believe that He created the world, or that He sent His Son, Jesus, to die on the cross. They may accept the fact that Jesus was a real person or lived on the earth and died on the cross or that the Resurrection really happened.

Think about your journey to belief in Christ. What were the first things you believed about Him? How strongly did you believe them? Which beliefs did you struggle with?

To be saved, however, a person must move beyond accepting the facts about God, though that is where faith begins (Heb. 11:6). Saving faith is believing that what God has done in Christ was done for you personally.

On one occasion, someone asked the Apostle Paul, "What must I do to be saved?" (Acts 16:30–31). Paul answered him by saying, "Believe in the Lord Jesus."

Belief is an action. We must choose to accept the gospel message as truth, and we must act on that choice by accepting it personally. Faith involves both an inward act of believing "with the heart" and an outward act of confession "with the mouth" (Rom. 10:8–10).

There came a time when you took this first step in the process of salvation. Once you made the choice to believe, your faith was strengthened by additional knowledge. Christ Jesus, your new friend, entered your life and now helps you grow. This is the way He wants it to be for you for your entire life, even after you have been a Christian for many years. You have embarked on the lifelong journey of faith.

Sorrow for Sin: Repentance

Genuine faith in Christ always includes a turning away from sin. That's called *repentance.* Both John the Baptist and Jesus began their ministries with a call to repentance (see Matt. 3:2; 4:17), and this call to repentance was at the heart of Jesus' mission (Luke 5:32).

To repent literally means to change one's mind. That change includes both our opinions and our intentions. Many people who have done wrong are sorry they were caught or that they had to suffer because of it. That is not repentance. Repentance includes two things: a confession of sin (Matt. 3:6; Mark 1:5) and a determination to change (Luke 3:4–14).

If there is no change in our lives, it's likely that we didn't really believe in Christ or accept God's grace in the first place. While faith alone is the condition of our salvation, the kind of faith that is necessary for salvation is faith that has a spirit of humility, of repentance. Without repentance, faith is merely intellectual assent; it is not a personal acceptance of God's grace. You might say that repentance is the evidence of our faith—it demonstrates that our belief in Christ is genuine.

Do you recall being sorry for your sins? What changes have taken place in your life as a result of your new faith?

What Happens When You Are Saved

So what happens when a person believes in Christ? The end of all true belief is salvation, or "being saved" from sin.

Sin has a claim on the sinner, and it bothers the conscience, separating the person from God. We cannot hide from God. And we cannot reform our lives to appease God. Only one hope is offered to us: forgiveness.

Forgiveness

Those who believe in Jesus are forgiven for their sins. The Bible says that "if we confess our sins, he is faithful and just and will forgive us our sins and purify us from all unrighteousness" (1 John 1:9). We can infer the same from Jesus' own words in John 8:24: "I told you that you would die in your sins; if you do not believe that I am the one I claim to be, you will indeed die in your sins" (John 8:24).

When we believe in Christ and repent from our sins, we are forgiven. Forgiveness is the initial experience of salvation.

Justification or Pardon

Yes, but can we—who are born as sinful people—ever be justified before God? We know that we can be.

There is a story in Luke 18:10–14 about a man who was truly repentant. The Bible says that, having confessed his sin to God, "he went down to his house justified." How is that possible?

Since we have sinned, we are guilty before God. But when God forgives us, He pardons us and makes us acceptable in His sight. Since Jesus took our guilt upon Himself and paid the price for our sin, we may receive a pardon.

> It is a wonderful thing to be justified before God. As the Bible says, we have peace with God through Jesus Christ our Lord.

Perhaps you can think of a time when you were guilty of doing something wrong. You may have tried to justify your actions by making excuses or blaming others, but in your heart, you know that it didn't work. You couldn't pardon yourself.

But when you asked God for forgiveness, a miracle took place. God, who alone can forgive sins, really did forgive you and make you "right" with Him.

It is a wonderful thing to be justified before God. Now you are not condemned but have God's favor. You are delivered from the guilt, penalty, and slavery to sin. No longer do you stand before the judge as a convicted criminal. Instead, you have a new relationship with God. You are reconciled to Him. As the Bible says, we have peace with God through Jesus Christ our Lord (Rom. 5:1–2).

The New Birth: Regeneration

Recall that when Adam and Eve fell, the image of God within them—and within us—was damaged. By regeneration, we are restored to a new likeness to God and a new relationship with Him.

In order for us to become children of God, a supernatural change must occur. We must be born again. This new birth—called *regeneration*—is not a second physical birth, but a birth of spiritual life. "I came that they may have life, and have it more abundantly," Jesus declared (John 10:10). This new life is a refreshing, cleansed, renewed life in the spirit. Jesus said, "Whoever hears my word and believes him who sent me has eternal life and will not be condemned; he has crossed over from death to life" (John 5:24).

Salvation is not simply deliverance from the threat of eternal damnation; it is salvation to a new life now—a life that pleases God and that is pleasing to us. We are

Christians not simply because we want to go to heaven but because the Christian life is the most satisfying, the fullest, the most joyful life one can possibly live. In fact, it is life as God intended it to be when He created human beings in the first place!

What Happens in Salvation	
Prevenient Grace	The Holy Spirit Draws Us to God
Faith	We Choose to Accept God's Grace
Repentance	We Are Sorry for Sin and Turn from It
Forgiveness	God Forgives Our Sin
Justification or Pardon	We Are Made Right with God
Regeneration	We Are Born Again, Made Alive in Christ
Adoption	We Are Included in God's Family
Assurance	God's Spirit Confirms That We Are Saved
Initial Sanctification	God Begins the Process of Cleansing Our Hearts

Adoption As a Child of God

Adoption is the act of receiving a stranger into the family and giving that person all the rights and privileges belonging to a natural child. Adoption is also a result of salvation. When you are saved, you are adopted into the family of God.

The supreme right that Christ gives to those who take Him as Savior and Lord is the right to become *children of God* (John 1:12). God created us, so we already have a relationship with Him as creature to Creator. One result of salvation is that we may enter a new relationship with God as child to Father. When we believe in Jesus Christ, we are acknowledged to be children of God, entitled to all the privileges of His children.

By the way, all of these things—forgiveness, justification, regeneration, and adoption—happen at the same time. Whereas justification is a legal term, adoption is a relational term. It implies more than pardon for sin; it expresses a covenant relationship. The Bible says, "God sent His Son, born of a woman, born under law, to redeem those under the law, that we might receive the full rights of sons" (Gal. 4:4–5). And "to all who received him, to those who believed in his name, he gave the right to become children of God" (John 1:12).

Since you are a believer in Christ and have repented of your sins, you are truly a child of God. "You did not receive a spirit that makes you a slave again to fear, but you received the Spirit of sonship. And by him we cry, 'Abba, Father.' The Spirit himself testifies with our spirit that we are God's children" (Romans 8:15–16).

Which aspect of salvation is most meaningful to you? Why?

Knowing That You Are Saved

Have you been saved from sin? How do you know? Can you be sure that you are now a member of God's family?

Yes, you can be sure. You don't need to guess about whether or not you've been forgiven and have eternal life. You have the assurance of God's presence and approval.

Here are two experiences that are evidences of our salvation.

The Witness of the Spirit

The Holy Spirit will reward a believer's search for assurance of salvation by a divine perception. This is more than human intuition; it is a direct divine illumination (John 20:27–29). The Holy Spirit creates an awareness within us that we have accepted Him and that He has accepted us. Our faith leads to a sense of "peace with God" (Rom. 5:1).

Nations at war know when they are fighting and when they are at peace. So it is with our relationship with God. We know when we are at war with Him, and we know when the war is over. "The Spirit himself testifies with our spirit" (Rom. 8:16). This assurance is not secondhand or suggested by our Christian teachers and preachers; it is an inner, personal persuasion created by the Holy Spirit Himself.

This is deeper than intellectual understanding. Frankly, no one can explain how this "testimony by the Spirit" is made apparent to the heart, but it is. The Holy Sprit gives every believer an assurance of his or her adoption by God.

Awareness of Change

A person who has been born again knows himself to be different from what he was. He can say, "Something has happened to me. I'm not the person I was." Salvation brings a religious and moral change in us. We have a new attitude toward God; we are alive to spiritual things. Also, there is a moral difference in the way we live; we have a new set of standards for making choices.

Some observable evidences of this change are that we have a new determination to obey God, we make a radical break with the old life, and we have our lives reoriented toward God and spiritual things.

So then, we know that we have peace with God both by the inner witness of the Spirit and by honest self-examination. As the Bible says, "Examine yourselves, to see whether you are in the faith; test yourselves. Do you not realize that Jesus Christ is in you—unless, of course, you fail the test?" (2 Cor. 13:5).

What changes have you seen in your life since you became a Christian?

What Comes Next

Knowing that you are a Christian brings a wonderful sense of peace. But God did not save us in order to leave us where we are. He has a plan for each of our lives, and that plan includes our growth as individuals and our service to Him.

Initial Sanctification

The kingdom of God, according to Paul is "righteousness and peace and joy in the Holy Spirit" (Rom. 14:17). Christ bore our sins, not as a substitute for our righteousness, but "that we might die to sin and live to righteousness" (1 Pet. 2:24). God intends for us to actually live a new and different life after we're saved. It is

God's intention to "make us holy through and through" (1 Thess. 5:23).

When we were born again, there was a new life created in us. We were changed, cleansed, made holy. But that cleansing is not complete. Our entire sanctification (holiness)—which is the state of being separated from all uncleanness and set apart for God—will be accomplished at some point in our lives by the work of the Holy Spirit. That process begins at the moment of our new birth. Self-centeredness is still present to some degree even in a person who has been born again. The uncleanness acquired through years of living apart from Christ is real, but we receive an initial cleansing, or sanctification, at the moment we're saved.

> God's work—making your holy—has begun in you. What He has begun in you, He will continue throughout all of your life if you remain obedient to Him.

Remember, it was a process of God's grace that led you to the point of believing in Christ and repenting of your sins. That process never ends. God's work—making your holy—has begun in you. In the future, you'll face significant experiences that will bring a deeper cleansing in your life. What He has begun in you, He will continue throughout all of your life if you remain obedient to Him.

Witnessing

If a person staggered into your room and informed you that the building would be blown up in five minutes, what would you do? It's possible that you might thank him for the information, tell him that you believed him, and then quickly show him to the door. If you were still in the building five minutes later, however, he could rightly conclude that you really had not believed him at all.

Likewise, you might claim to believe that Jesus Christ is the Savior of the world, that life's full meaning can only be realized through Him, and that apart from Him all people are under the threat of eternal damnation. But if you continue to live as before, never telling anyone the good news of salvation, nobody would put much stock in your claim.

If we genuinely believe the gospel, then nonbelievers will see a commitment to that truth in our everyday living. People who do not know Christ need to see the reality of genuine Christian experience in our lives. Only then will they be convinced by our words about Jesus Christ and what it means to know Him personally. As you

Five Principles for Witnessing	
Cultivate Social Contacts	Make a conscious effort to be with non-Christians. Witnessing to church folk will not win the lost.
Establish a Common Interest	Begin where their interests lie. Spiritual matters need not be the first subject of conversation.
Don't Condemn	Be a good listener. Understanding a nonbeliever is not the same as condoning his or her behavior.
Stick with the Main Issue	Refuse to be sidetracked by controversial issues. Focus on the truth of the gospel.
Confront Directly	At some point, present the claims of Christ and challenge the nonbeliever to make a decision. Saving faith, not mere friendship, is the goal.

Perhaps the best way to tell others about salvation is to relate your own experience—your testimony. You can witness—share your faith with others—simply by telling them what God did in your life through Jesus Christ. You will learn more about how to do this in chapter 4.

And witnessing goes beyond what we say. It includes all that we are and, therefore, all that we do. When you live your life for Christ, others will take note of your example. As you are faithful to Him, your life will be a witness to the good news.

Have you told anyone about your new faith in Jesus Christ? Who is the first (or next) person with whom you will share the good news about salvation?

To Learn More

God's Loving Plan for Your Future by Jerry Brecheisen

Taking the Truth Next Door by David Faust

Becoming a Contagious Christian by Bill Hybels and Mark Mittelberg

Ten First Steps for the New Christian by Woodrow Kroll, Tony Beckett, and Elisabeth Elliot

I Believe: Now Tell Me Why edited by Everett Leadingham

All additional books and resources are available from Wesleyan Publishing House at www.wesleyan.org/wph or by calling 800.4.WESLEY.

Personal Spiritual Journal

DATE _____

_____

_____

_____

_____

_____

_____

_____

_____

_____

_____

_____

_____

_____

My Prayer Today—

_____

_____

_____

_____

CHAPTER 3

Knowing God through His Word

Scripture

All Scripture is God-breathed and is useful for teaching, rebuking, correcting and training in righteousness, so that the man of God may be thoroughly equipped for every good work.

—2 Timothy 3:16–17

 **Bible Basics**

2 Timothy 3:14–17

[14]But as for you, continue in what you have learned and have become convinced of, because you know those from whom you learned it, [15]and how from infancy you have known the holy Scriptures, which are able to make you wise for salvation through faith in Christ Jesus. [16]All Scripture is God-breathed and is useful for teaching, rebuking, correcting and training in righteousness, [17]so that the man of God may be thoroughly equipped for every good work.

 Connecting God's Word to Life

What uses for the Bible do you see in this Scripture? List some ways that you use the Bible in your church and in your personal life.

A Unique Book

The Bible is a unique book. There is nothing like it for helping us know God and understand how to please Him. The Apostle Paul gave the Bible the highest possible compliment when he called it "God-breathed." He assigned to it the noble task of preparing God's people to declare the gospel. He couldn't have been more right about this book. Nothing else does for us what the Bible does. When necessary, it touches those areas of our lives that disappoint our Heavenly Father. In fact, it does more than touch. If allowed, it can slice like a scalpel, removing sin from our lives.

The Bible was one of the first books to be printed and remains the best-selling book of all time. In this chapter, we will learn why Paul believed it to be inspired, and we'll trace its fascinating development from the ancient world to your hands. Then we'll discover how you can get the most from the Bible so that you, too, will be "thoroughly equipped for every good work."

How We Know the Bible Is True

To say that the Bible is God-breathed is to make an astounding claim. The term *God-breathed* (or *inspired*) conjures an image of God breathing life into the book as He did into Adam at Creation. This means that God was ultimately responsible for producing the book and that it continues to have meaning. Other books begin to be obsolete immediately after they are written. To say that the Bible is God-breathed implies it will always be true and always effective.

When Paul made this claim, he was talking about the Old Testament, the first thirty-nine books of the Bible. Several things brought him to this conclusion.

Why We Trust the Old Testament

In Paul's day, the Old Testament was the Bible of the Jews. The Jews are a race of people chosen by God about two thousand years before the time of Christ. God revealed Himself to the Jewish people at many times and in various ways. The Jews wrote down what God said and did. They believed that what they were writing was not merely their own interpretation of God's words and actions, but was an inspired account of who He is. Over a span of nearly a thousand years, the Jews collected these writings and used them as their Bible.

The Words Came From God

The first leader of the Jews, Moses, gave many instructions to the people, including the Ten Commandments. He made it clear that what he commanded was not his own idea, but God's. Prophets like Moses often introduced their messages with the phrase, "This is what the LORD says." According to the Jews, the books of the Bible that do not specifically claim inspiration have demonstrated their divine origin in other ways; they contained fulfilled prophecies or agreed with books known to be inspired.

Some books were recognized as inspired very soon after they were written. The Israelites understood immediately that they must obey the commands that God gave through Moses. Daniel understood Jeremiah's prophecies to have come from

> Prophets like Moses often introduced their messages with the phrase "This is what the LORD says."

God, although the men lived at nearly the same time. Some books took longer to be accepted, but the Old Testament was essentially complete by about 100 B.C.

It Was Accepted by Early Christians

The very first Christians were Jewish, so they used the Old Testament as their Bible. As the church grew, it came to include people who were not Jewish (called *Gentiles*). They too accepted the Old Testament as their Bible. After all, Jesus had considered the Old Testament to be inspired. When He was confronted by His enemies, Jesus turned to the Old Testament for the final answer (see Matt. 4:1–11 and Mark 7:1–13). All the authors of the New Testament books shared Jesus' high respect for the Old Testament. Peter said about it, "The word of the Lord stands forever" (1 Pet. 1:25).

It's a Completely Reliable Book

The Old Testament has a unity that could not have been created by any human being. Although the books come from many different authors with many different perspectives, purposes, and styles, all of them agree on who God is and what He is doing.

> The Old Testament has a unity that could not have been created by any human being.

Many predictions are made in the Old Testament that are later shown to have been fulfilled. For example, it was predicted that the Jews would become slaves in Egypt, then be liberated and given the land of Canaan. Those events took place several hundred years later. It was also predicted that the Jews would go into exile because of their disobedience but would be allowed to return home by a king named Cyrus. Again, it happened exactly as predicted.

Early Christians also noticed that certain events which took place in their own day had been predicted in the Old Testament. The prophets said that the Savior would be born to a virgin in Bethlehem, that He would proclaim the good news about what God was doing, enter Jerusalem in triumph, be betrayed by a friend, and be killed for our sins. Jesus' life and ministry fulfilled each of those predictions. And on more than one occasion, Jesus stated that the Old Testament had spoken about Him (read Luke 24:13–35).

Why We Trust the New Testament

For the first several decades after Jesus, the early Christians were content to use the Old Testament as their Bible. As the church spread, however, leaders like Paul wrote letters to the Christians for whom they had responsibility. These letters were collected and treasured; copies were circulated among the churches.

Eventually, stories of Jesus' life were collected, written down, and circulated. We know these collections as the *Gospels*. Luke, one of Paul's associates, wrote a sequel to his Gospel, which recorded the history of the early church. This book was called The Acts of the Apostles (usually shortened to Acts). Together, these books came to be regarded as inspired, just as the Old Testament was, and became known as the New Testament.

It Was Selected by Early Christians

As with the Old Testament, the process of selecting the books for the New Testament was based on the collective opinion of God's people over a long period of time. First, the early Christians wanted to know whether a book was written by an apostle or his associate. Then they carefully considered what it said. Was it true? Did it contain fulfilled prophecies? Did it agree with other books that were considered inspired?

Within about two hundred years after Jesus' time, the church had agreed that the twenty-seven books of the New Testament were inspired. That decision was made official about two hundred years later. Since then, Christians have agreed that both the Old Testament and New Testament are "God-breathed."

It Has Internal and External Confirmations

All available evidence confirms the decision of the early church. No merely human book can match the Bible's content in unity and truth. No other book can boast so many fulfilled prophecies. No other book has accomplished what the Bible has accomplished.

To make the matter even more certain, God puts His stamp of approval on the Bible. He does this for each one of us, in our hearts, by His Holy Spirit. We recognize its truthfulness when God applies it to our lives, teaching and correcting us, training us to be godly people. When you have experienced God personally applying His Word to your life, you will understand for yourself that it is true.

Reasons to Believe the Bible Is Inspired
1. It claims to be inspired
2. Jesus said it is inspired
3. Its prophecies have been fulfilled
4. Its message is consistent throughout all books
5. It has had a great impact on civilization
6. The Holy Spirit reveals to us that it is inspired

Do most people you know think the Bible is inspired by God? Do you? Why or why not?

Why the Bible Is Important

The Bible profoundly impacts our lives for at least four reasons.

It Is God's Word

First, God has spoken through this Book. Other books might tell the truth, but only one communicates all the truth that we need to live a godly life. We can confidently form our understanding of God from what we learn in the Bible. It is the only authorized biography of God!

Also, we can form unchanging standards of right and wrong from the Bible's pages. In it we have an accurate description of the history of the universe, of humanity, and of how God brought salvation to the world. The Bible describes the future and gives an accurate view of who we are as human beings. Many books have been written about people, but only one by their Creator.

God Continues to Speak through It

Since God inspired the Bible, He *still* speaks through it to His people. When you read this chapter, you will "hear" me speaking to you, but with significant limitations. I will not be present when you read these words, nor will I speak personally to you.

When you read the Bible, God is able to speak directly to you through His Holy Spirit. You may not hear Him every time you open the Bible, and you probably won't hear an audible voice. If you listen, however, God will apply His Word just to you. He may want to teach you something. He may rebuke and correct you for some shortcoming. Or He may train you to become more righteous. Because the Bible is God's Word, it still speaks to those who listen.

It's a Training Tool for Christians

If you are a follower of God, then you are serious about obeying His commands. Learning lessons from God is similar to learning lessons at school—instruction is never easy! But as sincere followers of God, we humble ourselves and accept God's instruction, correction, and rebuke. Since the Bible is God's Word to us, it is our primary training tool, and we accept its message, even when it's challenging.

It Is God's Gift to Us

If you received a personal letter from a famous person or world leader, would you need to be prodded to read it? Of course not! You would probably tear open the envelope and carefully read every word. You and I have been given an even more precious gift. God has sent us a message. Not only that, but He comes along with it to help us better understand it. We should eagerly read and study the Bible to learn what He has to say.

Describe a time when you felt that God was speaking to you through the Bible.

How We Got the Bible

Since the Bible is God's Word, we want to understand it thoroughly. Reading the Bible can be intimidating, however. It's a very long book. The events described in it took place a long time ago and in a faraway land, and the plot can be difficult to follow. That's why it's helpful to understand something about the background of the Bible—how it was written and how it came to be in its present form.

Original Writings

Most of the Old Testament was written in the Hebrew language, which was spoken by ancient Jews. About three centuries before the time of Christ, it was translated into Greek to make it available to Jews who no longer spoke Hebrew. This translation of the Old Testament, known as the *Septuagint*, was the version of the Bible used by Jesus and the early Christians. Later, the New Testament, also written in Greek, was added to the Septuagint. Together, these books were circulated as the Christian Bible. Since the printing press had not yet been invented, all copies of the Bible were handwritten.

As the news about Jesus spread to other countries, it became necessary to translate the Bible into different languages such as Latin, Syriac, and Coptic. Wherever the good news traveled, translations were made into the native language of the land. With the development of the printing press in the 1400s, manuscripts could be mass-produced cheaper and much more quickly.

Eventually, new translations became necessary not only so the Bible could be read in new languages, but also so it could continue to be understood in languages that had changed over time. This was why the king of England authorized a new translation in 1611, which came to be known as the King James Version. New translations have been appearing in English and other languages ever since.

Major Translations of the Bible	
Version	**Date**
Septuagint (Greek Old Testament)	200–400 B.C.
Vulgate (Latin Bible)	A.D. 300–400
Luther's German Bible	1534
Tyndale's New Testament and Pentateuch	1530
Geneva Bible	1560
King James	1611
American Standard	1901
Revised Standard	1952
New American Standard	1971
Living Bible (Paraphrase)	1971
New International	1978
Good News	1979
New King James	1982
Contemporary English	1995
New Living Translation	1996
English Standard	2001

Many Translations

Translating any ancient book into a modern language is a tricky business. It is often impossible to find a word in the modern language that exactly matches the original word. Also, the meaning of any word depends heavily on the context in which it is used, but the context of the ancient writings is not always easy to determine.

The meaning of some languages, including English, depends heavily on the order of words in sentences. That is not the case for Greek and Hebrew. Translators face another problem with idioms and figures of speech. Should they be translated literally or not?

We have many different translations of the Bible, in part, because people have different opinions about how to go about

> We have many different translations of the Bible, in part, because people have different opinions about how to go about translating an ancient book.

translating an ancient book. Some people believe that a translation should match the original language as closely as possible, including exact matches of word meaning and word order, and literal renderings for figures of speech. These highly literal translations are more exact, but they are also more difficult to understand.

Other translators believe it's more important to represent the author's intended meaning rather than to precisely translate every word. These translators might change the order of words to more closely parallel English usage or substitute a figure of speech that is more common in our language. These translations are less precise, but they probably do a better job of conveying the overall meaning of a passage to the average reader. Versions of this type are sometimes called *paraphrases*.

Still a third group of translators uses a method know as *dynamic equivalence*. This method aims to balance the literal and paraphrase approaches. The result is a translation that is more readable than a literal translation but more exact than a paraphrase.

To illustrate the three types of translation, here are three versions of 1 Sam. 20:30.

Translation Theory	Version	Text of 1 Sam. 20:30
Literal	English Standard Version	Then Saul's anger was kindled against Jonathan, and he said to him, "You son of a perverse, rebellious woman, do I not know that you have chosen the son of Jesse to your own shame, and to the shame of your mother's nakedness."
Paraphrase	Contemporary English Version	Saul was furious with Jonathan and yelled, "You're no son of mine, you traitor! I know you've chosen to be loyal to that son of Jesse. You should be ashamed of yourself! And your own mother should be ashamed that you were ever born."
Dynamic Equivalence	New International Version	Saul's anger flared up at Jonathan and he said to him, "You son of a perverse and rebellious woman! Don't I know that you have sided with the son of Jesse to your own shame and to the shame of the mother who bore you."

The first is a more literal translation of the original Hebrew but is harder to understand. The second is very easy to understand. While not a word for word translation, it represents exactly what Saul was saying and the shock value he intended. The third translation strikes a balance between the two.

Choosing the Right Translation

As you can see, each type of translation has advantages and disadvantages. Each provides something that the others lack. Which one is right for you? It depends. If you are reading the Bible for the first time, choose a paraphrase, since it will be easiest to understand. For regular reading, a dynamic equivalence translation is probably best. If you are studying the Bible in depth, you may want the accuracy of a literal translation. If your pastor preaches from a particular version, you might want to choose that as your regular Bible. Most are now available with introductory notes on each book, commentary on difficult passages, and other reference material such as maps.

Comparison of Translations by Method		
Literal ← →	Dynamic Equivalence ← →	Paraphrase
King James Version New King James Version English Standard Version New American Standard Revised Standard Version New Revised Standard Version	New International Version New Living Translation Good News Bible New Jerusalem Bible	Living Bible The Message Contemporary English Version

Changing Languages

Translators must also contend with the reality that English, like all languages, is constantly changing. New translations must continually be produced so each new generation can understand what God is saying to it. Many Christians become attached to their favorite translation. Some go further and criticize other translations as unspiritual. Don't fall into this trap. Remember, each translation philosophy has value, and new translations are essential for allowing people to hear the Bible's message for themselves.

Which translation does your pastor use? Which type of translation seems most useful to you personally?

How the Bible Is Arranged

At any public library you'll find a wide variety of books: fiction, nonfiction, juvenile, poetry, reference, and many more. When you visit a library, it's helpful to know how the material is arranged so you can easily find what you're looking for. The Bible is like that. It's really a library contained in a single volume. It contains sixty-six books in at least eight categories of literature.

Knowing the Layout

The Old Testament comprises thirty-nine books, the New Testament has twenty-seven. Books of the Bible are divided into chapters and verses. The usual way of giving the address for a part of the Bible is to list the book, then the chapter number followed by a colon, then the verse number or numbers. For example, Matthew 4:1–11 means that the passage is in the book of Matthew, chapter 4, verses 1 through 11. You'll also see the names of the books abbreviated (for example, Matt. 4:1–11). There is a list of the books of the Bible and their abbreviations preceding the Scripture Index in this book.

> The Old Testament comprises thirty-nine books, the New Testament has twenty-seven. Books of the Bible are divided into chapters and verses.

The first five books are called the *Pentateuch*. They begin with the account of creation and tell the history of the Jews up to the point when they are about to enter the Promised Land.

Next come the historical books, which continue the history of the Jews from their entry to the Promised Land until about 400 B.C. The next section turns away from history to expose a poetic picture of life within Israel. The final section in the Old Testament contains the writings of the prophets.

The New Testament picks up the story about 400 years after the last events of the Old Testament. The first four books are known as Gospels. They tell the story of Jesus' life, death, and resurrection. The next book describes the early history of the church. A collection of letters follow, written by the Apostle Paul and other church leaders. The last book explains how Jesus will return to complete the work God began at Creation.

Here's an exercise to help you get to know the Bible: Review the table of contents in your Bible and find each book. You'll notice that some are very long while others are very brief, less than a single page. Read a sample of several books to note the different flavor of each writer.

Old Testament			
Pentateuch	**History**	**Poetry**	**Prophecy**
Genesis	Joshua	Job	Isaiah
Exodus	Judges	Psalms	Jeremiah
Leviticus	Ruth	Proverbs	Lamentations
Numbers	1 and 2 Samuel	Ecclesiastes	Ezekiel
Deuteronomy	1 and 2 Kings	Song of Songs	Daniel
	1 and 2 Chronicles		Minor Prophets:
	Ezra		Hosea, Joel, Amos,
	Nehemiah		Obadiah, Jonah,
	Esther		Micah, Nahum,
			Habakkuk, Zephaniah,
			Haggai, Zechariah,
			Malachi

New Testament		
Gospels	**Paul's Epistles (Letters)**	**General Epistles (Letters)**
Matthew	Romans	Hebrews
Mark	1 and 2 Corinthians	James
Luke	Galatians	1 and 2 Peter
John	Ephesians	1, 2 and 3 John
	Philippians	Jude
History	Colossians	
Acts	1 and 2 Thessalonians	**Prophecy**
	1 and 2 Timothy	Revelation
	Titus	
	Philemon	

Which book of the Bible seems most interesting to you? Why?

Knowing the Plot

Reading the Bible can be confusing because there are so many names, people, and places mentioned. But there is a connection between them!

As you find and follow that connection, your journey through the Bible's pages will be more enjoyable. Here's the story in a nutshell!

In the beginning, God created a perfect world, one in which each person felt at ease with God, with others, and with the natural world. Then disaster struck! Human beings disobeyed God. This act, sin, changed the world from a place where people felt at home to a place of violence, loneliness, and guilt. What did God do about this? That is the story of the rest of the Bible.

God's first step was to choose an older couple, Abraham and Sarah, and call them to leave their homeland and become nomads. In return, He promised them a homeland and many descendants. They had no children of their own, and Sarah was past childbearing age, but God gave them a son, Isaac. Through Isaac and his son Jacob, God brought many descendants, known first as Hebrews, then as Israelites, and finally as Jews.

God planned to use the Jews to save the world. The Old Testament tells how God made this family into a nation with its own laws, land, and leader. Unfortunately, they stumbled and disobeyed God. He had to discipline them, but He did not abandon them.

Finally, when the time was right, God sent His son, Jesus, into the world. He came as a baby, born to Jewish parents. He grew up and began to teach other Jews. He chose twelve men as His close associates, who were known as apostles.

Although the Jewish people gladly heard Him, their leaders were jealous and arranged to have Him killed. Little did they know that God would use Jesus' execution as the decisive blow against sin. On the third day after Jesus' death, God raised Him to life, proving His power over sin and sin's effects. The good news of Jesus' death and resurrection spread like wildfire among the Jews. Eventually, the message spread to the Gentiles and around much of the world.

While the Cross was the decisive moment, it was not the end of the battle. God continues to undo the effects of sin from the world. Much of what God is doing, we cannot see clearly. We do know that He wants to work through the Church. The Church is to model and proclaim the good news that sin no longer has the power to control and ruin us. We are to show that God's power is stronger and that His kingdom is growing. God did not leave the final victory up to us, however, but promises to intervene once again, finally and forever. Jesus will return and finish the work God started long ago.

> God did not leave the final victory up to us but promises to intervene once again. Jesus will return and finish the work God started long ago.

Using the Bible in Your Life

The Bible, like anything else, is most profitable when used for its intended purpose. So why did God give us this book? Although it can teach us how to live, how to be good parents, how to succeed in business, or what will happen in the future, these are not the primary reasons why God gave the Bible. He gave us this book so we could know Him. Therefore, the most important question to ask is always "What can I learn about God from this passage?"

Learning about God

You don't need to be a Bible scholar to ask this question, just keep your eyes open for four things.

1. *What the Inspired Authors Say about God.* For example, the Apostle John tells us that "God is love" (1 John 4:8).

2. *What God Says about Himself.* For example, we know that God never changes because He tells us so in Mal. 3:6.

3. *What God Does.* For example, we see that God is mighty and powerful when He parts the Red Sea.

4. *What God Doesn't Do or Say.* God never appears in the book of Esther, yet His people are spared a great tragedy. That shows that God can control circumstances without taking direct action.

Look for the characteristics of God that underlie His actions. Your goal is to know Him, not merely the things He has done. Also, compare what you learn about God in one passage with what you have learned about Him elsewhere in the Bible. You would not want people to base their opinion of you from only one action. In the same way, God reveals His character a bit at a time. Only by looking at the complete picture can we understand Him properly.

Memorizing Scripture

Once you learn something about God, hold onto it. Memorize passages from the Bible so you can recall these truths when you need them most. When you are frightened, you can remember that God is always present, as we see in Jesus' promise in Matt. 28:20, "And surely I will be with you always, to the very end of the age." When you feel overwhelmed by circumstances, you can remember that God is all-powerful, as Mary said, "Nothing is impossible with God" (Luke 1:37).

> Look for the characteristics of God that underlie His actions. God reveals His character a bit at a time.

Each of the chapters in this book features a key verse. Begin the habit of Bible memorization with these important verses. Use the flash cards at the end of this book as an aid to memorization.

Overcoming Temptation

As you get to know God through His Word, you will find it easier to say "no" when tempted to disobey Him. Not surprisingly, the serpent tempted Eve to disobey God by confusing her about what God had said and what He was like (read this fascinating story in Gen. 3:1–5). Nor is it a surprise that Jesus resisted Satan's temptation by quoting verses from the Old Testament that spoke about God's character (read Matt. 4:1–11).

As you learn God's Word, you'll gain strength to fight temptation.

Being Changed

The goal in knowing the Bible, of course, is grow in our relationship with God. God did not give us this book so we could study for a final exam. He told us what

He is like so we could know Him and become like Him.

The true test of our Bible knowledge, therefore, is not how well we recite facts, but how well we live. If we know that God is all-powerful, we will demonstrate that by trusting Him and being at peace in difficult circumstances. As we come to understand that God is merciful, we will put that knowledge into action by accepting His mercy when we stumble and showing mercy to others.

You have started on your personal journey of faith. To make the most of your trip, get to know the One who made this journey possible and who travels with you. He has revealed Himself to you through the Bible, so read it, study it, and put it to use in your life.

If you allow it, God will use His Word to teach you, train you, and correct you as needed so that you'll become a godly person, "thoroughly equipped for every good work" (2 Tim. 3:17).

What role does the Bible play in your life? List some benefits that you gain from knowing God's Word.

📚 To Learn More

How to Read the Bible for All Its Worth by Gordon Fee and Douglas Stuart
Reflecting God Study Bible
Wesleyan Bible Commentaries
Discover the Word edited by Everett Leadingham

All additional books and resources are available from Wesleyan Publishing House at www.wesleyan.org/wph or by calling 800.4.WESLEY.

Personal Spiritual Journal

DATE _____

_____

_____

_____

_____

_____

_____

_____

_____

_____

_____

_____

_____

My Prayer Today—

_____

_____

_____

_____

CHAPTER 4

Sharing the Good News with Others

Evangelism

> *"Come, follow me," Jesus said, "and I will make you fishers of men."*
>
> —Matthew 4:19

 **Bible Basics**

Matthew 28:18–20

[18]Then Jesus came to them and said, "All authority in heaven and on earth has been given to me. [19]Therefore go and make disciples of all nations, baptizing them in the name of the Father, and of the Son and of the Holy Spirit [20]and teaching them to obey everything I have commanded you. And surely, I will be with you always, to the very end of the age."

Connecting God's Word to Life

Matthew 28:18–20 is the Great Commission, our command to make disciples. Circle the action words in this passage. In what ways can you help to fulfill the Great Commission?

The Great Omission

Most Christians agree that we ought to share our faith story with others, but very few do. Some reports indicate that fewer than 10 percent of evangelical believers have ever led someone to the Lord. As one writer put it, "Christians and non-Christians have one thing in common: they're both uptight about witnessing!"

That reminds me of a story I heard about a group called The Happy Fishermen's Club. It seems that a group of avid fishermen decided to start a club. They elected officers and began holding weekly meetings to discuss the secrets of fishing. They would swap stories about the big fish that "got away" and talk about their next outing.

As the organization grew, they established a budget, wrote bylaws, and offered classes on the art of angling. They were enthusiastic about fishing, except for one obvious fact: they never caught any fish!

That's a snapshot of far too many churches when it comes to evangelism. We are mostly talk, very little action. These days, Jesus' command seems more like the Great Omission!

Go Get 'Em!

You Have the Right to Go Get 'Em—"All authority has been given to me . . ."

You Have the Responsibility to Go Get 'Em—"Therefore go and make disciples . . ."

You Have the Reason to Go Get 'Em—"And surely, I will be with you always . . ."

Why are some people reluctant to share their faith story? What would motivate you to be a more active "spiritual fisherman"?

The Right Attitude

If you plan to go fishing and want to actually catch fish, you need to know how to do it. Many people hate fishing because they tried it once without success. Perhaps they just didn't have the right attitude, knowledge, or equipment. Let's find out what it takes to be a successful spiritual fisherman, starting with the right attitude.

Visit a bait shop someday and ask the customers how they hope to fare. They will all say the same thing: "Today I'm going to catch a big one!" A good fisherman expects to catch fish.

Compare that with the attitude of the average Christian about evangelism. If you went to church and asked, "How will you do at making disciples this week?" the answer would likely be less enthusiastic.

> If you're going to catch fish, you'll need to learn how.

If we're going to bring people to faith in Jesus Christ, we must fully expect that our efforts will be successful, with God's help. Here are five elements of the right attitude for sharing your faith.

Concern for People

Every person you meet is important to God. He values each of us so much that He sent His only Son to die for our sins (John 3:16). Christ gave His life for us so we may have eternal life. If lost people are that important to our Heavenly Father, shouldn't they be important to us?

Knowledge of Eternity

If we believe in eternity, that belief will affect they way we life. If we genuinely believe that lost people are headed for hell, then we will be motivated to rescue them. Our belief about the eternal destiny of lost people will make a difference in the way we relate to them. Knowledge of eternity will motivate evangelism.

Reliance on the Holy Spirit

If God prompts you to share the faith with someone, it is because He is already dealing with that person. He is the first witness; you're always the second. Your words will simply confirm what the Holy Spirit is already doing. That's why you shouldn't feel anxiety about bringing spiritual things into a conversation. God is already suggesting them to the other person's mind! Just pray, listen to the Holy Spirit, and speak when He tells you to. The results are always up to God.

> Christ gave His life for us so we may have eternal life. Knowledge of eternity will motivate evangelism.

Nonbelievers As "Pre-Christians"

Many Christians are afraid of nonbelievers. Longtime Christians usually have few friends who are unconverted. They are much more comfortable in the "Happy Fishermen's Club" than being out where the "fish" are.

Contrary to popular belief, nonbelievers are usually open to spiritual matters. They are happy to discuss the deeper issues of life—as long as they don't feel manipulated or belittled. Begin to see nonbelievers as seekers, as "pre-Christians." They are more approachable than you think!

Conversion As a Process

The traditional approach to personal evangelism emphasizes the urgency of making an immediate decision. One often-used technique begins with the question "If you died tonight, do you know for sure that you'd go to heaven?"

That approach is based on a valid notion—that we must never be complacent about evangelism. But it overlooks the fact that most people come to Christ as a part of a process. Think of the decision to accept Christ as a *sunrise* rather than a *light switch.*

> Consider This:
> What if lost people really want to receive Christ, they just don't know it yet?

A sunrise takes time. We say the sun has risen at 6:35 A.M., but it was getting light at 6:15 and lighter still 6:30. That's typical of the way people come to Christ. It's true that some people have "light switch" conversions (notably the Apostle Paul; see Acts 9:1–9). But faith dawns on most people more gradually.

Think of the spiritual journey as a continuum from –5 to +5.

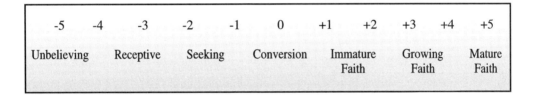

-5	-4	-3	-2	-1	0	+1	+2	+3	+4	+5
Unbelieving		Receptive		Seeking		Conversion		Immature Faith	Growing Faith	Mature Faith

When a person moves from –5 (nonbelieving) to –3 (receptive), your witness has been a success, not a failure!

Here's another analogy. Faith is like a growing seed. Often, one person plants the seed, another waters it, and a third harvests the fruit. In every case, it's God who caused the seed—faith—to grow (see 1 Cor. 3:6–9).

A word of caution is in order here. It is helpful to understand the process by which people often come to faith. But each person must reach a *moment of decision* for Christ at some point. Sadly, many churches are filled with nominal Christians—those who have been acclimated to the culture of Christianity, but have never experienced the power of conversion. Our goal is to make disciples of Christ, not simply to make new friends for ourselves.

List the three people you know who seem furthest from God. Pray for them every day and look for opportunities to move them "up the scale."

The Right Equipment

Any fisherman will tell you that if you want to catch fish, you need the right equipment. The most basic piece of fishing equipment is a pole. It's the foundation for most of the other fishing gear. In spiritual fishing, the starting point is a solid foundation of truth.

The Pole: A Foundation of Truth

In our desire to reach lost people, we must remain faithful to the truth. Against the tide of secular culture, we must stand strong and contend for the faith, presenting the gospel honestly—even if it offends some.

The Bible says that the Cross is a stumbling block for many. In other words, there are people who will be offended by the idea that they have sinned against God and need to repent, or that believing in the death and resurrection of Christ is the only way to be forgiven.

No matter. We must not water down our message in order to make it palatable to others. The full gospel is the only good news—the only hope—they have!

The Hook: God's Inspired Word

It is important to bring God's Word into your conversations with nonbelievers. As you show them that the Bible relates to their problems, they will come to see that it contains the answers for life's ultimate issues. Without the power of God's Word, we merely spout our own opinions. With the Word, we are armed for spiritual warfare (Heb. 4:12).

Evangelist Bill Fay uses the Bible in an interesting way when he shares his faith. He opens the Bible with a seeker and asks, "What does this verse say?" After the person reads the verse, he asks, "What does that verse mean?" In this way, sincere inquirers lead themselves through the plan of salvation!

The Line: Relationships

Very few people come to Christ outside the context of a personal relationship with a believer. "Pre-Christians" want to see if the Christian faith is for real. They observe the manner in which we live, watching to see if we're authentic.

Use the Book as the Hook!

Our lifestyle and our relationships with others are a central part of our witness for Christ. As St. Francis said, "Preach Christ at all times—when necessary, use words." It really is true that "people don't care how much you know until they know how much you care."

List three friends who seem to be seekers of truth. Name one thing you can do to build a stronger relationship with each person.

A Good Fishing Spot

You can't expect to catch any fish if your line is in a backyard bucket. You have to go where the fish are. Jesus showed that He was willing to go where the "fish" were when He said, "The Son of Man came to seek and to save that which was lost" (Luke 19:10). He went after lost people!

Have you ever wondered why the ratio of converts to church members is so low? One reason is that we fail to go after the fish. We hold meetings and expect the lost to come to us—but the Great Commission says we're to *go* to them! Instead of being fishers of men, we have become keepers of the aquarium.

So, how can the church meet lost people where they are? Here are four good fishing spots.

Their Point of Need

When people are hurting, they look for help. That's why Jesus did so much healing during His ministry. He connected with sinners at the level of their pain. He brought healing—and salvation!

Their Life Transitions

Most people are open to spiritual matters during life's transition points—marriage, childbirth, death, the empty nest, divorce, relocation.

Their Interest Level

Is there a hobby or interest you have that could be shared with a "pre-Christian" friend? A point of common interest is a great place to begin building a relationship.

Their Turf, Not Ours

Many Christians have little contact with nonbelievers. We don't run in the same circles. But Jesus said to *go* and make disciples. Find ways to bring the gospel to others—where they are.

What are the greatest needs in your community? What might your church do to bring the gospel to others while meeting those needs?

The Right Bait

Not all fish will bite on the same kind of bait. Fishermen select the bait depending on the type of fish they're after. In the same way, different kinds of "pre-Christians" will respond to different approaches to evangelism.

A few years ago, many Christians were encouraged to memorize a one-size-fits-all presentation of the gospel. "Don't let them deviate from the plan!" the soul winning instructors insisted. They forgot, however, that not all people have the same outlook or temperament, and not all people will respond to the same presentation of the gospel. When presenting the gospel, we'll need to vary the approach—but never the message—according to the situation.

Jesus' own ministry is an example of this. He didn't use a canned sales pitch, but He did have a consistent message! Consider the ways that Jesus varied His approach depending on the audience.

Jesus' Approaches to Sharing the Good News		
Person	**Scripture**	**Approach**
The Samaritan Woman	John 4	On her turf; used the task she was doing
The Thief on the Cross	Luke 23:43	Transition point; responded to a direct request
The Disciples	Matt. 4:19	Their interest level; used various settings and situations to teach them
Nicodemus	John 3	His interest level; answered his questions
The Scribes and Pharisees	Matt. 23	Their turf; used Scripture and the setting when they asked
The Woman Caught in Adultery	John 3:3–11	Her point of need; offered her forgiveness and correction

Who are the people you're trying to reach? What is the best way to reach them? Here are some different types of seekers and suggestions for attracting them to the gospel.

The Hurting

Many people are hurting, physically, emotionally, or spiritually. Their cry is "Heal me!" When we bring Christ to a hurting person, we must be soul doctors, tender and patient. We can bring them comfort from the Word and show them that Jesus wants to help them be whole.

The Angry

Others are angry about life and its injustices. Their cry is "Understand me!" Sharing Christ with a person who struggles with deeply rooted anger is a challenge.

It requires the gift of mercy and a willingness to listen. We can identify the inner pain that causes their hostility and show that Jesus can bring them peace.

The Intellectuals

Some people live by their intellect. Their cry is "Explain to me!" They're looking for a logical presentation of the gospel. The writings of authors like Josh McDowell, Lee Strobel, and C. S. Lewis are excellent "bait" for these rational thinkers who need reasons to believe.

> Who are the people you're trying to reach? What is the best way to reach them?

The New-Agers

In our pluralistic age, many believe that two seemingly contradictory ideas can both be accepted. Their cry is "Show me!" They need to be shown why competing truths cannot both be true. And they need to be shown that the false hope offered by New Age philosophies cannot compare with the spiritual intimacy of knowing Christ.

The Religious

Religious people cry, "Move me!" These folk have been raised in religious traditions that now seem dead. They need to see that there is more to faith than empty religious practices. They need to feel the power of an authentic relationship with the living God.

The Rebellious

In every age, there are rebels. Their cry is "Challenge me!" Their energy must be channeled in the right direction. They need a reason to live, something to live for.

The Willing

There are those souls who are ready and willing to know the truth. Their cry is "Teach me!" How wonderful it is to find people who are open and ready to receive God's truth. They need careful instruction, clear answers to honest questions.

The Audience	Their Cry
The Hurting	"Heal me!"
The Angry	"Understand me!"
The Intellectuals	"Explain to me!"
The New-Agers	"Show me!"
The Religious	"Move me!"
The Rebellious	"Challenge me!"
The Willing	"Teach me!"

Identifying Your Style

Fishing is a highly individualized sport. There are as many ways to fish as there are fishermen. Every avid angler seems to have his or her favorite combination of tackle, bait, and location.

Sharing the gospel is like that. You will develop your own style of relating the good news to others. God has wired us all to be different, and together we will reach many different people a variety of ways!

Here are several styles of faith sharing. See if one fits you.

The Logical Style

Some people like to memorize a plan and follow it to the letter. Does that describe you? If so, you'll probably be most comfortable developing a clear presentation of the gospel, probably one that uses Scripture quite a bit.

The Servant Style

People who use the servant style tend to be doers. They perform random acts of kindness in the name of Christ—mowing a lawn, helping a neighbor move, raking leaves for a single mom, or baking bread for a hurting friend. They gain trust in relationships, then move to share the good news.

The Testimony Style

Some people are natural talkers—especially about themselves! That trait can be useful in sharing the gospel, because each of us has a personal story of salvation. People who use this style tell their story of faith—their testimony—to others. A testimony has three basic parts:

- Part 1: What my life was like before I met Christ

- Part 2: My experience of coming to faith

- Part 3: The change that knowing Jesus has made in me

The Prophetic Style

Are you a no-nonsense person? Do you prefer to deal with people who speak plainly, whether it's comfortable or not? You may take to the prophetic style. Those who use this style of evangelism boldly proclaim the truth, regardless of opposition. They are unafraid to confront others with the claims of Christ.

The Listening Style

Are you empathetic? Do people say that you're a good listener? People who use the listening style of sharing the gospel are silent more than they speak. They direct a conversation by asking questions, helping the seeker to arrive at truth rather than pronouncing it.

> Some people are natural talkers. That trait can be useful in sharing the gospel, because each of us has a personal story of salvation.

The Resource Style

To use this style, share good books, CDs, tapes, or other items with your unsaved friends. Provide input that will spark their spiritual interest.

The Invitational Style

A simple way of presenting the gospel is to invite a nonbeliever to an event where the good news will be presented. You can practice this style by inviting friends to church, a Christian concert or film, or some other evangelistic event.

The Hospitality Style

Your social calendar can be a great evangelistic tool. Those who practice the hospitality style "do life" with lost people—they invite them to dinner, socialize together, and get to know them in non-threatening ways.

Chances are good that you will resonate with at least two of the above approaches. Celebrate your uniqueness! God knew exactly what kind of person you needed to be to reach the people He wants you to reach!

What is your style? Which of these approaches to evangelism fits best with your personality?

Landing the Catch

The most exciting moment on a fishing trip is when the fish bites. The bobber plunges under the water, and you know you've got a real chance to land a fish.

But you have to reel it in! Many fishermen have felt a tug on the line but failed to land the catch. Here are some tips for "setting the hook" in spiritual fishing—moving from relationship building to an actual presentation of the gospel that may lead to conversion.

Steering the Conversation

To present the good news, you must eventually move a conversation toward spiritual issues. God is preparing an opportunity for you to share your faith. Keep your eyes open for that.

Here are some questions you might use to steer a conversation toward spiritual matters.

- What is your anchor—the center—of your life?
- What are you hoping to do with the rest of your life?
- Besides having a lot of money, how would you define being rich?
- On a scale of 1 to 10, how important are spiritual things to you?
- Do you go to church? Why or why not?
- Do you pray? What do you pray about?
- If God asked, "Why should I let you into my heaven?" how would you respond?

Presenting the Message

Although a canned sales pitch is generally ineffective in presenting the gospel, it is very important to have a firm grasp of what the Bible says about salvation. Here are two well-known and effective outlines of the gospel message.

The Romans Road

- Rom. 3:23—All have sinned

- Rom. 6:23—All deserve death

- Rom. 5:8—God loves us, in spite of our sin

- Rom. 10:9, 13—Faith in Christ brings salvation

Steps to Salvation

- Step 1—God's Purpose: Peace and Life.

  God loves you and wants you to experience peace and life—abundant and eternal (Rom. 5:1; John 3:16; John 10:10).

- Step 2—The Problem: Our Separation.

  Sin separates us from God (Rom. 3:23; Rom. 6:23).

- Step 3—God's Bridge: The Cross.

  Jesus died on the cross and rose from the grave. He paid the penalty for our sin and bridged the gap between God and people (1 Tim. 2:5; 1 Pet. 3:18; Rom. 5:8).

- Step 4—Our Response: Receive Christ.

  We must trust Jesus Christ as Lord and Savior and receive Him by personal invitation (Rev. 3:20; John 1:12; Rom. 10:9).

Setting the Hook

In fishing, there is a moment when the fisherman must set the hook. When the fish bites, tugging on the line and pulling the bobber under the water, the fisherman must act quickly to pull on the line and hook the fish.

In spiritual fishing, there is a similar moment when you must "set the hook" by asking your nonbelieving friend to make a decision for Christ. God is preparing an opportunity for you to present the gospel in a clear and simple way. When that time comes, be bold!

It's likely that there will come a moment when the "bobber goes under" as your friend provides an obvious opportunity for you to present the truth. Be open to the Holy Spirit; He will let you know when that moment comes. Then it will be up to you to offer an opportunity to make a decision.

You might do that with a statement like this: "It seems like you are ready to place your faith in Christ. That's the greatest decision you could ever make. Would it be all right if I prayed with you right now to invite Jesus Christ into your life?"

> God is preparing an opportunity for you to present the gospel.

It's possible that your friend will decline your invitation to receive Christ. If that happens, don't pressure him or her—let the Holy Spirit continue His work. And don't take it personally. Remember, it's not you they are rejecting. You can rejoice that you have at least caused your friend to think about spiritual things. Pray that your encounter will move them a step or two closer to Christ.

More often than you think, the response to your invitation will be "Yes!" Be prepared to lead a brief prayer of confession, inviting your friend to pray along with you either silently or aloud. (There's about a 50 percent chance that the person will choose to pray silently, and that's OK.)

Finish your prayer by thanking God for the wonderful gift of salvation and the great things He is doing in your friend's life. Then rejoice together, and encourage him or her to tell someone about this decision.

Finishing the Job

The Great Commission does not instruct us to go and make *decisions* but rather to go and make *disciples*! The moment of decision is the beginning of a Christian's new life, not the end. Christ called us to teach converts to obey His commands (Matt. 28:19). So the work of the fisherman is not complete until the new believer has been involved with other Christians in the process of *discipleship*, or Christian growth.

Discipleship can take place in a variety of settings including Sunday School, small groups, and one-on-one mentoring. Regardless of the setting, the important thing is see that the convert is growing in the faith. Our job isn't finished until the new believer's life has been changed to become like Christ.

Here are some things you can do to help new believers start growing in the faith:

- Invite them to church.
- Involve them in your Sunday School class or discipleship group.

- Offer to meet with them again to talk about the Christian life.

- Introduce them to other believers.

- Suggest that they begin to read the Bible and pray daily.

- Offer Christian books, tapes, or literature.

Satan does not like to lose ground, and he will work overtime to discourage and defeat a new believer. It's vitally important that we finish the job of evangelism by involving converts in growing relationships with other believers.

Let's Go Fishing!

There is no greater joy in all the world than leading a friend to Christ. There are plenty of fish in the sea—people who need salvation—not only in your community, but around the world. If the Great Commission becomes a Great Conviction in our hearts, we will make a great difference for heaven's sake.

It's time to dust off the pole, pick up the bait, and go fishing!

What is the first thing you will do to start sharing the good news with others?

 **To Learn More**

Out of Their Faces and Into Their Shoes by John Kramp

Becoming a Contagious Christian by Mark Mittelberg and Bill Hybels

Steps to Peace with God by Billy Graham

A Case for Christ and *A Case for Faith* by Lee Strobel

The Master Plan of Evangelism by Robert Coleman

Mere Christianity by C. S. Lewis

More Than a Carpenter by Josh McDowell

How to Lead an Adult to Christ booklet

How to Lead a Child to Christ booklet

How to Lead a Teen to Christ booklet

Leading Your Grandchild to Christ booklet

EvangeCube

All additional books and resources are available from Wesleyan Publishing House at www.wesleyan.org/wph or by calling 800.4.WESLEY.

Personal Spiritual Journal

DATE _____

_____

_____

_____

_____

_____

_____

_____

_____

_____

_____

_____

_____

_____

My Prayer Today—

_____

_____

_____

_____

CHAPTER 5

Growing Deeper in the Christian Life

Holiness

It is God's will that you should be sanctified. . . .

—1 Thessalonians 4:3

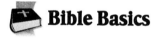 **Bible Basics**

1 Thessalonians 5:23–24

[23]May God himself, the God of peace, sanctify you through and through. May your whole spirit, soul and body be kept blameless at the coming of our Lord Jesus Christ. [24]The one who calls you is faithful and he will do it.

 Connecting God's Word to Life

What does the word holy suggest to you? List some people or things that you consider to be holy?

Trying to Live the Good Life

Have you ever tried to be good? I mean really good? Maybe as a kid, you tried to go for an entire day without picking on your sister. As you grew older, you may have tried to resist the temptation to lust or gossip. You determined that from that moment on, you were going to be really, *really* good.

How did it go?

I probably know the answer. We've all failed at living the good life.

Here's another question. Did that change after you became a Christian? When you decided follow Jesus Christ, did your behavior become perfect immediately? Was it instantly easier to do the right thing?

If you're like most people, you'll admit that you still struggle to live the good life, even though you're a believer. Being forgiven doesn't make you perfect.

That frustrating experience has led some to believe that holiness is an impossible dream. They conclude that only saints of long ago or maybe a few extraordinary people can live the good life, but you and I can't. Ordinary people simply can't be holy.

But the Bible presents a very different view of holiness, one that takes your struggle and failure into account. Scripture tells us that God wants you to be a different, better person than you are. It's His will that you should be sanctified—that is, made holy. And He has the power to do it. That's called *entire sanctification*, and here's how it happens.

Why It's So Hard to Be Good

As you already know, there's a problem with the good life. It seems that the harder you try to be good, the more difficult it becomes. What you're experiencing is the struggle against your sinful nature, and you're not alone.

The Battle with Self

The Apostle Paul was one of the earliest and most devout followers of Christ. He came from a religious home where he was taught to be obedient. After he met Jesus (see Acts 9:1–19), Paul became one of Christ's most ardent supporters and poured all of his energy into being a disciple. But even Paul, an apostle, faced this same struggle with sin. He confessed:

> [15]I do not understand what I do. For what I want to do I do not do, but what I hate I do. . . . [18]I know that nothing good lives in me, that is, in my sinful nature. For I have the desire to do what is good, but I cannot carry it out. [19]For what I do is not the good I want to do; no, the evil I do not want to do—this I keep on doing (Rom. 7:15, 18–19).

That aptly describes the experience of most people, even many Christians, when it comes to doing the right thing. We just can't seem to get it right.

Why? It's because of our *sinful nature* (Rom. 7:15).

Romans 7

Slavery to the Sinful Nature

Ever since Adam and Eve sinned in the Garden of Eden (see Gen. 3), human nature has been flawed. That *original sin* was passed on to all of Adam's descendants, including you and me. Although we are made in the *image of God* (Gen. 1:27), we are no longer able to glorify God fully because our very nature is corrupted by sin. Like a CD with a scratch on it, we simply can't reproduce the original—God's goodness—the way we should. Paul concluded sadly, "What a wretched man I am! Who will rescue me from this body of death?" (Rom. 7:24).

Have you ever felt that way?

Our Helplessness

That lament makes a vital point about our condition, and one that we too easily forget: we can't fix ourselves. Many people believe that doing the right things (and avoiding the wrong things) is a matter of willpower. That is, if we make the right resolves and try hard enough, we'll be able to overcome the sin nature within us. But that bootstrap spirituality simply doesn't work. The prophet Jeremiah put it succinctly: "Can the Ethiopian change his skin or the leopard its spots? Neither can you do good who are accustomed to doing evil" (Jer. 13:23). You can't change your basic nature, and your basic nature is sinful. Working harder just won't do it.

> God intends to do for you what you cannot do for yourself—transform you into the better person that you long to be.

God's Plan

Our situation isn't hopeless, however. The fact that you even desire to do right is a sign that God is at work in you. God put that longing in your heart. And He didn't give you that desire in order to make you frustrated and miserable. God fully intends to make you a new person (see 2 Cor. 5:17). In fact, the Bible explicitly states that "it is God's will that you should be sanctified" (1 Thess. 4:3) and adds, "The one who calls you is faithful and he will do it" (1 Thess. 5:24).

The word *sanctified* means *made holy*. Clearly, God intends to do for you what you cannot do for yourself—transform you into the better person that you long to be. But it will happen in His time and in His way, not through your own hard work.

In what ways have you felt like a slave to your sinful nature?

The Meaning of Holiness

So where does the journey to holiness begin? And where is it headed? What does it mean to be holy?

Ask two Christians what it means to be holy, and you're likely to get three opinions. Other than the end times, there's probably no subject that has aroused more debate than holiness. The word has a very simple meaning, however, and it's clearly defined in Scripture.

In the Old Testament, God called the Israelites to be His special people. They were set apart for a unique relationship with God. That made them holy (see Exod. 19:6; Deut. 28:9–10; 1 Pet. 2:9). So the first

> Consecrated means set apart.

meaning of the word *holy* is *set apart*, or reserved especially for God. By the way, it wasn't just the nation of Israel that was set apart as holy. Some individuals and even things were holy as well. The priests (Exod. 28:41), altar, washbasin, utensils (Lev. 8:11), and other articles (Num. 4:15) were reserved exclusively for use in the service of God. They were holy.

There is a term that describes the act of setting something apart for God. The term is *consecration* (see Exod. 29:1; 40:11). To consecrate something is to make it holy by dedicating it to God.

There is a second meaning for the word *holy*, and that is *pure*. Things (or people) that are consecrated to God must be purified. (Some examples of purification: of people, Exod. 19:10; of the altar, Exod. 29:36; of a house, Lev. 14:52; of garments, Num. 31:20.) The reason for this is simple: God does not accept unclean things. The Apostle Paul made that point when he quoted the prophet Isaiah: "Therefore come out from them and be separate, says the Lord. Touch no unclean thing, and I will receive you" (2 Cor. 6:17).

That may be the best one-sentence description of what it means to be holy: First, come out—that is, consecrate yourself exclusively to God. Second, touch no unclean thing—that is, be pure.

That's holiness in a nutshell: consecration and purity.

Holiness Equation
Consecration + Purification = Sanctification

How does this definition of holiness differ from your original notion? Based on this definition, what people or things do you know that are holy?

Our Part: Consecration

But how do I become holy? We've already discovered that we can't make ourselves holy. How does holiness become a reality in my life?

Of the two meanings of holiness—consecration and purity—one of them is something you can act on. That's consecration.

We've discovered that God is already at work in you, creating the longing for holiness. That's called *prevenient grace.* The fact that your heart longs for God—to know Him, to be accepted by Him, to be like Him—is His own doing. It's His desire that you should respond to Him.

You can respond by consecrating your life to Him. The Apostle Paul gave a blueprint for self-consecration in his letter to the Christians in Rome. He said, "Therefore, I urge you, brothers, in view of God's mercy, to offer your bodies as living sacrifices, holy and pleasing to God—this is your spiritual act of worship" (Rom. 12:1). In other words, our response to the grace of God should be to dedicate ourselves completely to Him. You can make your whole life a sacrifice to God.

The act of consecration is our part in the holiness equation. God has placed the longing for holiness within us. We can respond by offering ourselves completely to God.

Have you ever consecrated your life completely to God? I'm not talking about the time when you asked God to forgive your sins. As important as that moment is, it's not the same as consecrating your life to Him.

Most people, when they ask to be forgiven, are thinking more about the past than the future. They are humbly asking God to forgive the sins they have already committed—which He is always ready to do! (see 1 John 1:9).

Consecration is an act that looks toward the future. It says, "Here's my whole life, God. Here are my family, my future plans, my thoughts, and my career—everything that I have. I give them all to you."

Have you ever made a statement like that to God? What led you to consecrate your life to God, and what was the result?

God's Part: Cleansing

Consecrating your life to God is part of *sanctification* (being made holy). But there's something more, and that's being made pure. Yet just as the leopard is powerless to change its spots, you and I are unable to rid ourselves of the sinful nature. We can't purify ourselves, but God can, by the power of His Holy Spirit.

Some people doubt that human nature can be changed at all, even by God. But the Apostle John makes it clear that God intends to do exactly that. He wrote: "If we confess our sins, he is faithful and just and will forgive us our sins and *purify us from all unrighteousness* (1 John 1:9, emphasis added). God never intended only to forgive our past sins and then to leave us powerless to avoid sin in the future. His plan is to make a change in our hearts—to purge selfishness from them—so that we are able to fully love and serve Him.

The book of Hebrews uses an interesting image to describe that change. Quoting the Old Testament prophet Jeremiah, the writer says this: "The Holy Spirit also testifies to us about this . . . 'I will put my laws in their hearts, and I will write them on their minds'" (Heb. 10:15–16).

In other words, God intends to change our inner nature so that we will readily understand and gladly do His will. We will then be able to live the new and better life that we had previously been out of reach.

Can you see that principle in these two Scriptures? "[He] gave himself for us to redeem us from all wickedness and to purify for himself a people that are his very own, eager to do what is good" (Titus 2:14). "How much more, then, will the blood of Christ, who through the eternal Spirit offered himself unblemished to God, cleanse our consciences from acts that lead to death, so that we may serve the living God!" (Heb. 9:14).

God really can change your heart. He can make you what He wants you to be. That's the essence holiness!

The Holy Spirit's Role in Sanctification	
Lives within you	1 Cor. 1:6
Confirms salvation	Rom. 8:16
Washes	Titus 3:5
Cleanses	Heb. 9:14; 10:22
Purifies	2 Cor. 7:1; Titus 2:14
Sanctifies	Rom. 15:16
Brings Freedom from Sin and Death	2 Cor. 3:17; Rom. 8:13; Gal. 5:16
Teaches	John 14:26
Empowers	Acts 1:8; Rom. 15:19
Produces Virtue	Gal. 5:22–23; Rom. 5:13; 1 Thess. 1:5
Gives Gifts	1 Cor. 12:9; Heb. 2:4
Seals (Preserves)	Eph. 1:13; 4:30

The result of this change in our nature is what the Bible calls *life in the Spirit*. Just as we had a sinful nature, we can now have a nature that is controlled by the Spirit of God. Again, thanks to the Apostle Paul for making this crystal clear. It's worth reading what he said about the death of the sinful nature and the new life in the Spirit in Rom. 8:3–9, 13:

[3]For what the law was powerless to do in that it was weakened by the sinful nature, God did by sending his own Son in the likeness of sinful man to be a sin offering. And so he condemned sin in sinful man, [4]in order that the righteous requirements of the law might be fully met in us, who do not live according to the sinful nature but according to the Spirit. [5]Those who live according to the sinful nature have their minds set on what that nature desires; but those who live in accordance with the Spirit have their minds set on what the Spirit desires. [6]The mind of sinful man is death, but the mind controlled by the Spirit is life and peace; [7]the sinful mind is hostile to God. It does not submit to God's law, nor can it do so. [8]Those controlled by the sinful nature cannot please God. [9]You, however, are controlled not by the sinful nature but by the Spirit, if the Spirit of God lives in you. . . . [13]For if you live according to the sinful nature, you will die; but if by the Spirit you put to death the misdeeds of the body, you will live, because those who are led by the Spirit of God are sons of God.

Fabulous! The old you, the one that was powerless to do the right thing, is put to death, gone. By the Spirit of God, you are set free! You are now able to live a completely different life. The Holy Spirit cleanses your heart so that you can live the good life that you have longed to live.

Romans 8

Freedom
in the Spirit

What areas of your life have been cleansed by the Spirit?

When Sanctification Happens

Wait a minute. Can holiness really be that simple? If holiness is possible, how come I'm still struggling with sin?

In reality, people generally are not transformed in an instant. While those overnight revolutions can happen, most people grow into the experience of holiness over a period of time. Here's how most people experience the holy life.

Initial Sanctification

The fact that you even want to be holy is important. Have you ever noticed that many people don't? They seem quite happy living according to their sinful nature. Their lives are focused on themselves, and they think that's OK.

But you're different. You have a desire to please God. Why?

As we've noted, that's because God has already begun to work in your heart. We've called that *prevenient grace,* and what that grace accomplishes is your *initial sanctification.* You might think of this as God planting the seed of holiness in your heart. He turns your heart toward Him, giving you the desire to be something different than you are. That happens when you trust Him for salvation—He begins, or initiates, your sanctification. You experienced initial sanctification when you became a Christian, part of the family of God.

Progressive Sanctification

After that, most people experience a period of gradual growth in their spiritual lives. Over time, they begin to live the Spirit-controlled life that Paul described in Rom. 8. Old habits gradually fall away, and the Spirit-filled person becomes more and more able to love God.

But why doesn't it happen all at once? If God wants to cleanse my heart, why does it take so long?

The primary reason for that is our failure to respond fully to the Holy Spirit. God is always ready to give us more than we are ready to receive. It's not until we're fully consecrated to Him that we can be fully cleansed.

The best example of that principle is the Israelite people who wandered in the desert for forty years waiting to enter the Promised Land. They were led by the Spirit of God the entire time (see Exod. 40:34–38), and they could have entered the Promised Land much sooner than they did. God was ready, but they weren't. At every turn, they seemed to be stubborn and disobedient. It took forty years to shape them into an obedient people. Only then were they ready to enter Canaan. (See Num. 32:13; Deut. 8:2; Heb. 3:7–12).

> God is always ready to give us more than we are ready to receive. It's not until we're fully consecrated to Him that we can be fully cleansed.

Most people experience something like that in their spiritual lives. For example, you may come to a moment of consecrating your life to God. But will you comprehend the scope of that? Will you realize all that's involved? Most people don't, at least not right away.

You might picture it this way. Consecrating your life to God is like inviting someone to be a guest in your home. As a generous host, you might say, and really mean, "Make yourself at home. My house is your house." But if you discovered your guest poking around in your bedroom closet, you might take offense. "Well I didn't mean *there!*"

You were sincere when you said "Make yourself at home," you just didn't realize how literally your invitation might be taken.

Consecrating your life to God can be like that. You think you mean "everything," but in reality, there may be things you're not ready to surrender—your career plans, perhaps, or your thought life, or your children's education, or your finances. In the back of your mind there may be one or two areas that are still off limits to God.

Over time, the Holy Spirit will reveal these holdout areas to you. As you surrender them, you will more fully understand what it means to consecrate *everything* to God, and you'll gain even more power to live a changed life.

That process is called *progressive sanctification*. It is the process of becoming fully consecrated to God and fully cleansed of the sinful nature.

There are lots of Scriptures that describe this growth in the Spirit. (For example: Eph. 4:14–15; Phil. 1:9–11; 3:13–16; James 1:1–4; 1 Pet. 2:2; 2 Pet. 1:5–8). Perhaps the best picture of what that looks like comes from Paul's letter to the Christians in Philippi:

> [9]And this is my prayer: that your love may abound more and more in knowledge and depth of insight, [10]so that you may be able to discern what is best and may be pure and blameless until the day of Christ, [11]filled with the fruit of righteousness that comes through Jesus Christ—to the glory and praise of God (Phil. 1:9–11).

That's a snapshot of progressive sanctification. Does that describe you?

Entire Sanctification

Is it possible to be fully sanctified? Can I ever get to the place where I am entirely consecrated to God and my sin nature is completely renewed by the Spirit? Yes. That's called *entire sanctification*, and the Bible teaches that it can be a reality for every believer.

> Consecrating your life to God is like inviting someone to be a guest in your home. "Make yourself at home. My house is your house."

The Bible says, "May God himself, the God of peace, sanctify you through and through. May your whole spirit, soul and body be kept blameless at the coming of our Lord Jesus Christ. The one who calls you is faithful and he will do it" (1 Thess. 5:23–24). Clearly, God intends to sanctify us (make us holy) completely. And again, "Do not conform any longer to the pattern of this world, but be transformed by the renewing of your mind. Then you will be able to test and approve what God's will is—his good, pleasing and perfect will" (Rom. 12:2). So God expects that changed behavior will become a reality—not simply an ideal—in our lives. God truly intends for us to live lives that are pleasing to Him.

That experience comes when we have fully consecrated ourselves to God and He has fully cleansed our sinful nature. From that moment, we are able to serve God with a fully obedient heart. We no longer willfully disobey God, but are able to walk in complete obedience to His will. That victorious experience should be the burning desire of every believer. As Jesus said, "Blessed are those who hunger and thirst for righteousness, for they *will* be filled" (Matt. 5:6, emphasis added).

After the moment of entire sanctification, we continue to grow in grace and obedience. Just as people who are adults continue to grow wiser (and older!), sanctified believers continue to mature in the Christian life. The moment of entire sanctification represents a milestone, not a stopping point.

Freedom from Sin

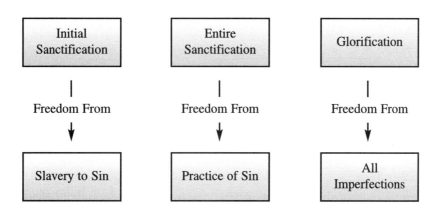

Initial Sanctification	Entire Sanctification	Glorification
Freedom From	Freedom From	Freedom From
Slavery to Sin	Practice of Sin	All Imperfections

Glorification

Of course, the ultimate perfection of our nature will take place in heaven. That's what we're all really hungering for—the final transformation of body, mind, and spirit (Phil. 3:20–21). That's called *glorification*, and that's when our sanctification will really be complete.

As long as we live, we're subject to temptation and failure. Even a person who has surrendered him- or herself completely to God may inadvertently break God's law or cause harm to someone else. Having perfect intentions is one thing; perfect execution of those intentions is something else entirely. Although we may act in good faith, as long as we're human beings we'll be limited, ignorant, and prone to mistakes. Sanctification doesn't change that.

In heaven, however, we'll be fully changed to be like Christ. There, the full effects of sin will be eliminated (see Rom. 8:19–21; Rev. 22:3). So it's important to remember that heaven—and the glorification that it brings—is our ultimate goal.

Of the three stages of sanctification — initial, progressive, and entire — which one best describes your life right now?

What a Holy Life Looks Like

So what does a holy person look like? As I am sanctified, what changes will I see in my life?

Victory over Sin

One result of sanctification—whether progressive or entire—is a growing victory over sin. Those who live by the Spirit find that they're increasingly able to act on what before were only good intentions. They begin to win that battle with the sinful nature that Paul talked about (see Rom. 7:7–25). "So I say, live by the Spirit," Paul later wrote, "and you will not gratify the desires of the sinful nature" (Gal. 5:16).

Maturing Christians find that doing the right thing (and avoiding the wrong things) comes more and more naturally to them. What once were areas of habitual failure gradually become areas of habitual victory. Finally, they are able to live lives that are free from purposeful disobedience to God's will. Their lives are characterized by the fruit of the Spirit: love, joy, peace, patience, kindness, goodness, faithfulness, gentleness, and self-control (Gal. 5:22–23).

Walking in the Spirit

Love of Others

Another term that's sometimes used for holiness is *perfect love.* That's because when God cleanses our hearts, we begin to love Him and others in a more mature, unselfish way. Do you remember Paul's prayer for the Philippian church? He prayed that their "love may abound more and more" (Phil. 1:9).

People who are progressing in sanctification will become less selfish and more attuned to the needs of others. That attitude is summed up in Paul's command to "do nothing out of selfish ambition or vain conceit, but in humility consider others better than yourselves" (Phil. 2:3).

Mature Christians display a mature love for others.

Active Service

Remember that to be holy means to be set apart for use by God. Sooner or later, God will put a holy person to good use!

Empowered by the Holy Spirit, maturing Christians will be at work, using their God-given abilities for the benefit of others (see Rom. 12:3–8; 1 Cor. 12:12–31; Eph. 4:11–16). Often, the most mature people in a congregation will be the most active—praying, teaching, contributing money, taking care of the sick. God seldom takes a consecrated vessel and puts it on the shelf. Consecrated people are most often put to work serving those around them. You may find a spiritual gifts test and personality profile helpful as you begin actively serving the Lord (see the To Learn More section).

Have you discovered your spiritual gift? What will you begin doing to use your gift?

Continual Growth

One of the most significant characteristics about people who are holy is that they don't think of themselves as perfect. The Apostle Paul set the standard for this when he said: "Not that I have already obtained all this, or have already been made perfect, but I press on to take hold of that for which Christ Jesus took hold of me" (Phil. 3:12).

Imagine! Paul was one of the godliest people of his day, or any other. Yet he was modest about his own spirituality and a need for constant growth. That's common among true saints. They're never interested in talking about their achievements and seldom set themselves up as examples. Instead, they make it their aim to offer their lives to God continually—to be living sacrifices (Rom. 12:1).

What changes have you seen in yourself since you've been walking in the Spirit?

Common Questions about Holiness

The idea of being made holy is nothing new, of course. The concept is mentioned over and over in Scripture, and it's always been the growing experience of sincere Christians—even some who don't believe it's possible! Yet some believers have trouble understanding the notion that God can make people holy, perhaps because it sounds presumptuous on our part. Here are some common questions people ask about the holy life.

Does being sanctified mean that I'll never be tempted?

No. Even Jesus was tempted (see Luke 4:1–13). Our human needs and desires don't disappear when we consecrate ourselves to God. Satan continues to present opportunities to gratify those desires in selfish ways. But by the power of God's Holy Spirit, we're increasingly able to resist the Devil and be guided by the Spirit (see Rom. 8:1–11). If anything, those who are mature in the Spirit are more keenly aware of their own temptations—and more on guard against them.

Sin and Sanctification				
	Sin Nature	**Progressive Sanctification**	**Entire Sanctification**	**Glorification**
Relation to God	Opposed	Turned Toward	Close Fellowship	Present With
Possible to Sin?	Yes	Yes	Yes	No
Possible to Avoid Sin?	No	Yes	Yes	Yes
Experience	Habitual Sin	Growing Victory Occasional Disobedience	Habitual Victory Unintentional Error	Perfection

Is it possible for a sanctified person to live without sinning?

First, let's define the term *sin*. The best definition is this: Sin is known disobedience to the known will of God. In other words, to sin is to do something intentionally that you know is wrong. And yes, it is possible for a sanctified person to live without choosing to disobey God.

But remember, we'll always be liable to make mistakes, which are not properly called sins. Here's an example. Suppose that you're driving to the store and doing your best to be careful. But you are momentarily distracted by your child calling to you from the back seat. In that instant, you inadvertently exceed the speed limit by one mile per hour. Did you break the law? Yes. But was it intentional? No. And it's unlikely that a judge would find you guilty for an honest mistake of that kind.

In the same way, a sanctified person may occasionally make mistakes, errors in judgment, and the like. Being holy doesn't mean you're not human! But in God's sight, it's the condition of your heart that really matters. Jesus made that point emphatically in His Sermon on the Mount (see Matt. 5–7). He stressed that it's the heart (the will, or intention) that makes any action good or evil (see especially Matt. 7:15–20). The sanctified person has a heart that is fully devoted to doing God's will; it is therefore free from sin.

Is a truly holy person beyond the point of sinning?

No. No one is beyond temptation or so far advanced in the spiritual life that sin is not possible. People who are growing in sanctification may, in fact, willfully sin. They will likely repent of it quickly and return to walking in step with the Spirit (Gal. 5:25).

Even those who are entirely sanctified could sin. You can probably think of a time when you heard a very mature person say something rude or selfish. It surprised you, perhaps, and seemed sadly out of character, but it happened nonetheless. In the same way, an entirely sanctified person could succumb to temptation and willfully do wrong. This side of heaven, we'll always be liable to sin.

What is the importance of intention in determining whether an action is sinful?

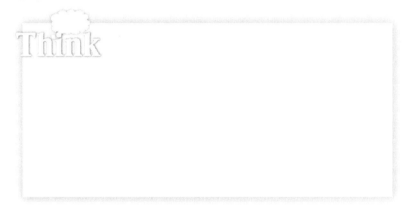

106

To Learn More

Whatever Became of Holiness: The Urgency of Holiness in a Postmodern World by Steve DeNeff

More Than Forgiveness: A Contemporary Call to Holiness Based on the Life of Jesus Christ by Steve DeNeff

Holiness for Ordinary People by Keith Drury.

A Plain Account of Christian Perfection by John Wesley.

Called to Be Holy by John Oswalt

Keys to Positive Relationships (a personality profile)

Spiritual Gifts Inventory

How to Live the Holy Life edited by Everett Leadingham

Filled to the Brim and *FAQs about the Spirit Filled Life* brochures

All additional books and resources are available from Wesleyan Publishing House at www.wesleyan.org/wph or by calling 800.4.WESLEY.

Personal Spiritual Journal

DATE _____

_____

_____

_____

_____

_____

_____

_____

_____

_____

_____

_____

_____

_____

My Prayer Today—

_____

_____

_____

_____

CHAPTER 6

Learning to Put God First

Worship

Let everything that has breath praise the LORD. Praise the LORD.
—Psalm 150:6

 **Bible Basics**

Psalm 150:1–6

¹Praise the LORD. Praise God in his sanctuary; praise him in his mighty heavens. ²Praise him for his acts of power; praise him for his surpassing greatness. ³Praise him with the sounding of the trumpet, praise him with the harp and lyre, ⁴praise him with the tambourine and dancing, praise him with the strings and flute, ⁵praise him with the clash of symbols, praise him with resounding cymbals. ⁶Let everything that has breath praise the LORD. Praise the LORD.

 Connecting God's Word to Life

As you read the above passage, note the variety and intensity of ways in which we are told to worship God. How is your worship similar to this description? How is it different?

God First

The struggle between human beings and God has always concerned the issue of control; that is, who is in charge of your life, you or God? The first pages of the Bible reveal that Adam and Eve's original sin was committed precisely because of their desire to be in control. When God said, "Don't," Adam and Eve said, "We will if we want to!"

Worship is the act of putting God first in your life. In this chapter, you will learn why worship is important for a Christian and how you can worship in daily life. As you learn to "bow the knee" to God, acknowledging His lordship over the world and yourself, your life will take on new meaning and you will discover the joy of exalting Christ.

Corporate Worship

Throughout the history of God's people, there have been two general contexts for worship: public or corporate worship, and private or personal worship. Let's examine corporate worship first.

The New Testament is filled with examples of corporate worship, occasions when people gathered to honor God through song, testimony, prayer, preaching, and teaching. The writer of one New Testament book challenged the people of God to "not give up meeting together" (Heb. 10:25). This is God's way of telling you that your life will be enhanced by regularly gathering with like-minded followers of Christ.

First Corinthians 12 shows us that each part of Christ's "body" has value to the others. Corporate worship allows us to function as a body. It enables us to meet each other's needs to a greater degree than if each of us interacted with God only in private.

Activity

Corporate worship can be formal or informal. It may include a good deal of liturgy (structured participation by the congregation), or it may be laid-back and casual. Scripture does not prescribe the level of formality that should be applied to a worship service. It does, however, suggest

> Each part of Christ's "body" has value to the others. Corporate worship allows us to function as a body.

elements that should be included in corporate worship.

Here are some biblical elements of corporate worship:

- Music (Ps. 92:1; 96:1; Eph 5:19)

- Prayer (Acts 1:14; 2:42)

- An affirmation of faith (1 Cor. 15:3–5, now such as the Apostles' Creed)

- Personal testimonies (1 John 1:1–3)

- Giving tithes and offerings (Deut. 16:17; Mal. 3:10; 1 Cor. 16:1–2)

- Baptism (Acts 16:13–15)

- The Lord's Supper (1 Cor. 11:17–26)

- Scripture reading (Luke 4:16–21; Acts 2:42)

- Preaching (Acts 8:4; 15:35)

This list demonstrates the variety of ways in which a group might express its love and devotion to God and His Kingdom. Each element contains its own potential for variety and intensity of expression.

Variety

There may be more than one mode of expression for any element of worship. For example, there is tremendous variety in the music used in churches today. Some use instruments; others don't. Some use an organ only; others add a piano, guitar, or drums. And the type of music used in church may range from chants, to hymns, to choruses.

Variety may be seen also in the practice of prayer in different churches, or even within a congregation. Prayer may be offered silently, read aloud, or given extemporaneously.

Even the sacraments, baptism and communion, may be observed in a variety of ways. Baptism may be administered by immersion, sprinkling, or pouring. And the Lord's Supper may be received while seated, standing, or kneeling.

There really are many ways to express praise and thanks to God. Every congregation probably has a favorite way of approaching God, but it's refreshing to try new things in corporate worship.

Intensity

Not all of the words you say are spoken with the same intensity. A rousing "Hurray!" shouted at a sporting event will be spoken with more energy than an "I love you" whispered to a loved one. Both are sincere expressions of emotion, but they vary in intensity.

In the same way, the intensity of corporate worship may vary according to the occasion. We may be quiet, reflective, jubilant, weepy, remorseful, or grateful at different times. At some times, a slow, moving musical piece may communicate the mood of our worship. At another time, the crash of a cymbal offered in praise to God might be more appropriate.

In the Bible you will observe physical expressions of worship such as hand clapping, bowing, dancing, and lying prostrate before the Lord. Prayer, too, may vary in intensity, sometimes being offered quietly—even silently—and at other times being spoken with tears.

All of these expressions are acceptable and meaningful when done unto the Lord. It is important to note that God calls all of it a "joyful noise" (even if it's not exactly on key!).

Two Styles of Modern Worship		
	Formal	**Informal**
Atmosphere	Often quiet, reflective	Often celebratory, "noisy"
Music	Primarily hymns	Primarily choruses
Prayers	May be written	Usually extemporaneous
Instruments	Organ and piano, primarily	Guitar, drums, electronic keyboard
Affirmation of Faith	By recitation of creeds	By personal testimony
Sermon	Delivered from a manuscript	Delivered from an outline or notes

Do you prefer a formal or informal style of corporate worship? Why?

Private Worship

Private worship is personal worship—it's done solo, just you and God. It's important for each of us to have a daily time with God, encountering Him in the midst of daily living.

The New Testament shows that Jesus had a private time with His heavenly Father, often early in the morning. In Ps. 5:3, David expressed a desire to meet with the Lord each morning to "lay my requests before you, and wait in expectation." Genesis tells us that Adam, the first person in the world, walked with God each day, enjoying fellowship and closeness with his Creator.

Find some quiet time each day to spend alone with God, talking, singing, listening, weeping, or rejoicing. It may last an hour or only fifteen minutes. Length is not as important as depth. The purpose is to connect with God through worship—to know Him better and to love Him deeper.

> Be still and know that I am God.
> –Psalm 46:10

Scripture gives little detail on how to fill this daily time with God. Therefore, people have developed a variety of activities to aid in this God encounter. Certainly, Bible reading and prayer will be essential for your personal worship. Here are two "user-friendly" methods for structuring your personal prayer time.

The ACTS Method

One method suggests the use of four elements in daily prayer that form the acronym ACTS.

- *A—Adoration.* Begin your prayer time by expressing worship and love to God and Christ.

- *C—Confession.* Allow the Spirit of God to explore your weakness and sinfulness. Confess your sin to God and receive His forgiveness.

- *T—Thanksgiving.* Say thank-you to God for His goodness to you.

- *S—Supplication.* Ask God for His help. Make your requests known to Him and let Him know that you trust Him to meet your need.

The Lord's Prayer

Another simple plan for daily prayer uses the Lord's Prayer as a guide (see Matt. 6:9–13). Jesus' classic prayer included statements on these elements:

- *Adoration.* "Our Father in heaven, hallowed be your name."

- *Subjection.* "Your will be done on earth . . ."

- *Requests.* "Give us today our daily bread . . ."

- *Confession.* "Forgive us our debts. . ."

- *Reconciliation.* "As we have forgiven our debtors."

- *Strength.* "Lead us not into temptation . . ."

- *Protection.* "Deliver us from the evil one . . ."

Remember that there is no single correct formula for moving closer to God. In fact, it is good to simply be silent before the Lord periodically. To realize one's daily dependence upon God can be a most empowering experience.

What are the benefits of having a daily time with God? List some things that can interfere with having this regular time with God.

The Theology of Worship

The biblical words for worship refer to the act of bowing down, or prostrating oneself, before another more worthy person. The basis of our worship is our belief that Jesus Christ is Lord and that God's will is to be desired and obeyed.

When you read the Bible, you will find that worshiping God has always been a central activity for His followers. In the book of Revelation, there are many references to God being constantly worshiped in heaven (see Rev. 5:8, 9; 11:16–18; 14:3 and 15:3, 4). In the Old Testament Temple, the people offered sacrifices of worship to God at various times throughout the year. When Mary, mother of Jesus, found out that she was pregnant with God's Son, she cried out in a song of worship (see Luke 1:46–55). The book of Acts describes the early Church's passion for worship (see Acts 2:42–47; 16:25).

Beginning with the time of Moses, we can see four distinct periods in the life of God's people, each with its own style of worship.

Time Period	Place of Worship
Wilderness wanderings	A moveable Tabernacle
Occupying the Promised Land	A permanent Temple
The scattering of the Jews throughout the world	A local synagogue
The early Christian church	House churches

Source: *The New International Dictionary of the Bible* (Zondervan Publishing House, 1963).

Places of Worship

First is the Old Testament period of the *Tabernacle*. The Tabernacle was a meeting tent that the Israelites used for worship as they traveled throughout the desert.

The second period began when the Israelites built a permanent worship structure called the *Temple*. Here, the worship experience became highly structured.

> To worship means to ascribe worth or value to someone or something. "Great is the LORD and most worthy of praise."

The third period was defined by the use of the *synagogue*. This institution was developed by Jews who lived in exile. Synagogues were constructed wherever Jews lived. Synagogue activity centered on instruction more than on worship.

Fourth is the New Testament period of the *house church*. Early Christians gathered to worship, typically in someone's home.

Our modern period began when Christianity was recognized as a legal religion in the fourth century A.D. During this time, the first buildings for Christian worship were erected. Worship again became very ritualized, using symbol and written word to guide the worshiper.

The Meaning of Worship

Our word *worship* is derived from the old English term *worth-ship*. To worship really means to ascribe worth or value to someone or something.

Jack Hayford, in his book *Worship His Majesty*, suggests three questions to assist the worshiper in determining the worth of that which is worshiped.

- What value do you place on this act? Is the manner of honoring the One being worshiped proportional to His character?

- Do the praises of the worshipers indicate their awareness of the traits inherent in the object of their worship?

- Does the worship involve genuine devotion, or is it only intellectualized? Is it worship in truth, but not in spirit? Does the worship come from the heart?

Theology is never meant to be a "stand-alone" pursuit; it is not an end in itself. A theology of worship, therefore, should lead us to a deeper appreciation for the One being worshiped.

First Chronicles 16:25 states, "Great is the LORD and *most worthy* of praise" (emphasis added). Jesus told His followers that whoever wishes to be a worshiper must "worship in *spirit* and in *truth*" (John 4:24, emphasis added). Christ's statement implies an integration of theology and feeling, intellect and heart. The biblical stories of how people worshiped "back then" were written to inspire our worship today.

The Purpose of Worship

Why is it so important that we worship God? What is the point of our worship? Our worship has at least five aims—five results it will produce in our lives and in our relationship with God.

To Ascribe

The first purpose is to ascribe worthiness to God. He alone desires your worship and affection. His position as Creator of all things gives Him the right to be worshiped.

To Align

Worship's second purpose is to align ourselves with the will of God. Jeremiah 29:11 states that God has a plan for each person's life. Through worship we surrender our will for ourselves to His will for us.

To Acknowledge

To acknowledge our total dependence upon God is the third purpose of worship. Until one realizes his or her total dependence upon God—for this life and for eternal life—that person will never fully attain to the "abundant life" that Jesus promised. Scripture tell us that "God inhabits the praises of His people" (Ps. 22:3). When we worship God, we invite Him into our daily existence. Proverbs 3:6 tells us that if we are willing to acknowledge Him, He will "make our path straight." Worshiping God affects the direction of your life!

> "God inhabits the praises of His people" (Ps. 22:3). When we worship God, we invite Him into our daily existence.

To Admit

The fourth purpose is to admit our sinfulness and our need for forgiveness. The Bible tells us that we have all "fallen short" (Rom. 3:23), that we are "dead in our sins" (Eph. 2:1), and that we need to be "born again" (John 3:3). When we confess our sin to God, He will faithfully and lovingly forgive us and cleanse us from guilt (1 John 1:9). That is accomplished through worship. It is when we worship that we admit our need for forgiveness and receive God's pardon.

To Admire

Fifth, we worship to admire God's constant involvement in our life. You don't need to look far to see God's fingerprints on your life. He has been good to you; He has protected you. He has given you wisdom when called for, and He has generously given you everything you have needed to enjoy this life. In other words, He has lovingly protected you as His precious child. The act of worship allows you to say thank-you to your Heavenly Father, to bless the One who has so richly blessed you.

Human beings (that's you and I!) were created to worship. That is why we often run wildly in pursuit of other things and other people. We are trying to satisfy our need to ascribe value to something or someone other than ourselves. Jesus acknowledged this tendency in Matthew chapter 6. In verse 33, He lovingly tells His followers to seek His kingdom *first.*

Which of the five purposes for worship comes most naturally to you? With which do you struggle? Why?

The Act of Worship

In the dictionary, *worship* is listed first as a noun. We usually think of worship as a thing. But worship is primarily a verb—it's something you do! It is an action of the heart. It is the primary act for which you and I were created.

In the Garden of Eden, our first parents chose to take their own path. They chose to take their way instead of God's. Ever since that fateful moment, the human heart has been restless. The act of worship is the secret to our contentment. "Bowing the knee" before almighty God is a wonderfully freeing act. This is the irony of worship. To submit oneself to God is to live in true freedom.

You *do* worship. The attitude of your heart ascribes worth or value to something or someone. When we choose to worship God, our outward actions expose the inner posture of our heart. The symbols of worship (lifting hands, kneeling, quietness, singing) are all expressions of a our deep passion, our submission, and our gratitude to a generous and awesome God.

 ## To Learn More

Up With Worship by Anne Ortlund

Whatever Happened to Worship? by A. W. Tozer

Worshiping God edited by Everett Leadingham

Worship Is a Verb by Robert E. Webber

All additional books and resources are available from Wesleyan Publishing House at www.wesleyan.org/wph or by calling 800.4.WESLEY.

Personal Spiritual Journal

DATE _____

_____

_____

_____

_____

_____

_____

_____

_____

_____

_____

_____

_____

_____

_____

My Prayer Today—

_____

_____

_____

_____

CHAPTER 7

Managing Your Life with God in Mind

Stewardship

Love the Lord your God with all your heart and with all your soul and with all your mind and with all your strength. The second is this: love your neighbor as yourself. There is no commandment greater than these.

—Mark 12:30–31

 **Bible Basics**

Jeremiah 1:5

> ⁵Before I formed you in the womb I knew you, before you were born I set you apart. . . .

1 Corinthians 6:19–20

> ¹⁹Do you not know that your body is a temple of the Holy Spirit, who is in you, whom you have received from God? You are not your own; ²⁰you were bought at a price. Therefore honor God with your body.

Ezekiel 18:4

> ⁴For every living soul belongs to me, the father as well as the son—both alike belong to me.

Connecting God's Word to Life

What value does your life have to God? Why did you answer as you did?

Not Our Own

We do not belong to ourselves. The Bible teaches us that we—and everything we have—belong to God. We are merely *stewards*, or managers, of our lives and possessions.

A steward is someone who acts as a supervisor of someone else's property. The concept of *stewardship* was established by God at the time of Creation. (See Genesis 1:26–31.) God created light and darkness, food to eat, air to breathe, and water to drink. He created plants, animals, birds, and fish—then He created human beings and gave them authority over all of creation. God even gave them stewardship over their own lives by creating them with a free will. Although people have abused that freedom and made selfish choices, God has never abandoned His creation, nor has He retracted His original appointment of human beings as stewards of His creation.

So what does stewardship mean for you and me? How do we go about managing God's creation? Being a good steward involves several things, and it begins with our attitude toward God.

My Life:
What Will I Do With It?

How can I glorify God?

What is God's place in my life?

Where does family fit in?

What should I do about serving others?

What about money and possessions?

Our Attitude toward God

"Love the Lord your God with all your heart and with all your soul and with all your mind and with all your strength" and "love your neighbor as yourself" (Mark 12:30–31). Those are the two greatest commandments in all of Scripture, according to Jesus. They form the foundation of the Christian life. It could be said that the rest of the Scripture is built on them.

This love for God was the prevailing attitude in the Garden of Eden before Adam and Eve disobeyed God's direct command. When they did, sin entered the world, and people began to love self more than God. Their souls were blighted by the disease of self-worship, their minds began to conceive all kinds of evil, and their energy was dedicated to self-preservation. The rest of the Bible tells of a God who never gave up on humankind and who instituted the plan of salvation that ultimately led His only Son to a cross. On that cross, He died to redeem lost people to Himself and restore the close relationship that was lost in the Garden, to make it possible to love God as we should.

The Great Commandment in Mark 12 is really a quotation from the Old Testament. It's taken from Deut. 6:5, where Moses gives his last instructions to the people, just before his death. It is not one of the Ten Commandments, but it summarizes them. It is as if Moses were appealing to the Israelites on a different level, calling them to elevate their understanding of God. After all, they'd had the Ten Commandments for almost forty years. Now, Moses challenged them to get beyond the do's and don'ts of the Law and obey God by choice, because they love Him.

That is what God wants for us today: not that we ignore the Commandments, but that we obey them out of our love for Him and desire to glorify Him. If we love God with all of our heart, soul, mind, and strength, and love our neighbor as ourselves, everything else will fall into place.

What do you think it means to love God?

Loving God, of course, is not hard to do. He is a loving and kind father, and there are many reasons to love Him with all of our being. Here are a few.

Love God	
Because of who He is	Isa. 40:25-31
Because He first loved us	1 John 4:19
Because of His grace and mercy	Rom. 5:8
Because of His gift of life and salvation	Eph. 2:8–9

Loving God for Who He Is

There is a great description of God found in Isaiah 40:9–31. Verses 25–31 are particularly important. It would be good to memorize these beautiful verses:

> [25]To whom will you compare me? Or who is my equal?" says the Holy One. [26]Lift your eyes and look to the heavens: Who created all these? He who brings out the starry host one by one, and calls them each by name. Because of his great power and mighty strength, not one of them is missing. [27]Why do you say, O Jacob, and complain, O Israel, "My way is hidden from the LORD; my cause is disregarded by my God"? [28]Do you not know? Have you not heard? The LORD is the everlasting God, the Creator of the ends of the earth. He will not grow tired or weary, and his understanding no one can fathom. [29]He gives strength to the weary and increases the power of the weak. [30]Even youths grow tired and weary, and young men stumble and fall; [31]but those who hope in the LORD will renew their strength. They will soar on wings like eagles; they will run and not grow weary, they will walk and not be faint.

The Bible contains many descriptions of God, but human language is really inadequate for this task. The best we can do is resort to words like infinite, omniscient (all-knowing), omnipotent (all-powerful), and omnipresent (all-present). God is so wonderful that it's difficult to describe Him!

God is the Creator of the universe (Gen. 1:1; John 1:1, 2). He is also our Father; we are adopted as His sons and daughters. As such, we are joint heirs with His Son Jesus Christ (Rom. 8:17).

Practically every page of the Bible contains some attempt to help us know God, to show us that He loves us, and to teach us how we may enter a relationship with Him. In fact, God is love (1 John 4:16).

Loving God Because He Loves Us

We love God because He loved us first. The Scripture tells us about God's love: "This is how God showed his love among us: He sent his one and only Son into the world that we might live through him. This is love: not that we loved God, but that He loved us and sent His Son as an atoning sacrifice for our sins" (1 John 4:9–10; John 3:16).

Loving God Because of His Grace and Mercy

The Bible tells us that we are all sinners (Rom. 3:23) and as such are under the penalty of death (Ezek. 18:20). But God loved us, even while we were still sinners, and He gave Himself for us (Rom. 5:8). We love God because He is gracious and merciful.

Loving God Because of His Great Gifts

The Bible clearly tells how we may be saved. Ephesians 2:8–9 explains that it is "by grace you have been saved, through faith—and this not from yourselves, it is the gift of God—not by works, so that no one can boast."

Jesus said: "I have come that they may have life, and have it to the full" (John 10:10).

God's great gift of love to us is the gift of eternal life through Jesus Christ, His Son, who gave us this assurance: "As the Father has loved me, so have I loved you. Now remain in my love" (John 15:9). We love God because He has been good to us.

We cannot save ourselves. By God's provision for our salvation we receive forgiveness for our sins, God's power to live the Christian daily, and the promise of eternal life with the Lord in heaven forever. Surely these are grand reasons for us to love God.

> Practically every page of the Bible helps us know God, shows us that He loves us, and teaches us how we may enter a relationship with Him.

In what ways do you demonstrate your love for God?

Our Treatment of Others

Managing our lives well begins with loving God. It includes our treatment of others also.

God created people for fellowship with Him. When He created Adam, God saw that Adam needed a companion. So God created Eve, intending for Adam and Eve to share their lives with one another. Human beings lived in perfect harmony not only with God but also with each other.

Sin changed that. The act of disobedience that separated Adam and Eve from God also drove a wedge between them. Blame and resentment entered the world. Human relationships have been marked by sin ever since.

But God had a plan. His plan to redeem the world included a plan to redeem human relationships as well. Because of Christ's death on the cross, we are reconciled to God, and we can be reconciled to each other.

Jesus is our example in this. He demonstrated the selfless attitude that brings us closer to one another when He said, "Even the Son of Man did not come to be served, but to serve, and to give his life as a ransom for many" (Mark 10:45). He did not live with the motto of "What is in this for me," but rather, "What can I give for the good of another." He even loved us so much that "while we were still sinners, Christ died for us" (Rom. 5:8).

Being stewards of God's creation means adopting this attitude of Christ and treating others as we would like to be treated ourselves (see Luke 6:31 and Phil. 2:1–11). The way we treat others is an indication of our commitment to Christ. It is the major way that people today can know that Jesus makes a difference in our lives and our relationships.

Treat Others . . .	
As you want to be treated	Luke 6:31
With kindness and forgiveness	Eph. 4:32
As valuable to us and God	Mark 12:31
With love	1 John 4: 7–12

Forgiving Others

Sometimes we demand too much perfection from others before we want to have a relationship with them. That's not the way God treated us. He knew that Adam and Eve would disappoint Him, but He created them, loved them, and shared life with them anyway. God never chooses to love for what it would benefit Him. He is always willing to forgive, and we should be too. As Paul said, "Be kind and compassionate to one another, forgiving each other, just as in Christ God forgave you" (Eph. 4:32).

Valuing Others

People are always more important than things. We live in a culture that evaluates a person's worth by the amount of his salary or the value of his car or home. When our values are driven by these external measures, it is easy for things to take precedence over people in our lives.

Even though the things and activities in our lives may be legitimate—jobs and homes, for example—we must remember that people matter more. Jesus placed the needs of other people ahead of His own. He healed the sick, fed the hungry, and tolerated the faults and foibles of His disciples. He valued people, and He called us to do the same (Mark 12:31). We are to treat others as valued children of God.

Loving Others

We are called by God to model His love to those around us. In 1 Cor. 13, which is sometimes called the Love Chapter, the Apostle Paul describes what it means to love others. We are to treat others with kindness, patience, not envy them or their possessions. We are not to boast, display rudeness, nor to be self-seeking, not be easily angered, nor should we keep a record of those who have wronged us. We are to rejoice with the truth. We are to protect, always trust, always hope, and always persevere. Love never gives up!

This kind of love may not be an automatic response, even for a Christian. But with God's help, we can treat others with respect and love. Don't stop trying or become discouraged when you fail in this area. God will help you to love others—even your enemies!—as you seek His direction.

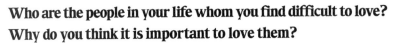

Why It Matters

In 1 John 4:7–12 we are commanded by God to love one another, and we are told that the world will know we are Christians by our love. John tells us that love is the hallmark of a Christian—not the way we dress, not the rules we keep, not the church we attend, not by how much we give, although these may be important.

If we are to manage our lives with respect for God, we must love and forgive others. People matter to God, therefore they must matter to us too.

Our Use of Things

Perhaps the most obvious area in which we are to be stewards of God's creation is in the use of our money and possessions. As believers in Christ, we manage our money with God and eternity in mind. The Lord gives us Matthew 6:20 as a guide for the use of things. We need to discover ways we can store up treasures in heaven rather than simply earn money on earth. Investments for eternity pay the greatest dividends.

What the Bible Says About . . .	
Money	Matt. 6:24
Tithe	Mal. 3:10
Dangers of wealth	Mark 10:25
Money to benefit others	1 John 3:17

The Value of Money

Jesus had a great deal to say about money and possessions. In Luke 12:15 we read, "A man's life does not consist in the abundance of his possessions." In other words, there's more to life than having things!

When God was dealing with the rich farmer who devoted all of himself to his business interests, He told him, "You fool! This very night your life will be demanded from you. Then who will get what you have prepared for yourself? This is how it will be with anyone who stores up things for himself but is not rich toward God" (Luke 12:20–21). When we realize that our lives will end someday, a right relationship with God and others seems much more important than accumulating wealth. In fact, money often distracts us from being fully devoted to God. As Jesus said, "You cannot serve both God and Money" (Matt. 6:24).

Possessions are only a means to an end. We use them to glorify God and to do His will. Since everything we have belongs to God, we should consider what He wants when making decision on the use of our money.

The Tithe

One way of honoring God with our possessions is to give Him a *tithe*, meaning one tenth, of our income. This biblical guideline dates to the Old Testament (see Gen. 14:20; 28:22) and has long been the standard for supporting the Lord's work (see Mal. 3:10). By giving one tenth of our income to God, we demonstrate that we trust Him to provide for us and that we believe His work is important.

> By giving one tenth of our income to God, we demonstrate that we trust Him to provide for us and that we believe His work is important.

As a practical matter, it's important that we contribute to the church because its funding depends on the gifts of its members. If we don't support the church, who will?

The Dangers of Wealth

There is not a set of rules for how many possessions one may accumulate; that is something we each must work out with the Lord. The Bible tells us that the love of money is the root of all kinds of evil (1 Tim. 6:10). Ecclesiastes 5:10 says, "Whoever loves money never has money enough; whoever loves wealth is never satisfied with his income. This too is meaningless." And Jesus warned that it is difficult for a rich person to enter the kingdom of God (Mark 10:25).

Although most of us do not think we are wealthy, we live in a prosperous age and enjoy many benefits of wealth. Remember, though, that we depend on God, not money, for our security.

Using Money to Benefit Others

It is a wonderful blessing to be able to give our selves and our possessions to meet the needs of others. The Apostle Paul instructed the Corinthian Christians in 2 Cor. 8:7, "But just as you excel in everything—in faith, in speech, in knowledge, in complete earnestness and in your love for us—see that you also excel in this grace of giving." In 1 John 3:17 we read, "If anyone has material possessions and sees his brother in need but has no pity on him, how can the love of God be in him?"

Seeing the many people who suffer from hunger and want, one might be tempted to cry out, "Where is God? Why doesn't He do something?" Yet it may be that God looks at the same needs and asks, "Where are my people? Why don't they do something?"

God has given the world to us, and everything in it. Being good managers of His wealth involves using our resources to help meet the needs of others.

What is your opinion about tithing, that is, giving one tenth of your income to the Lord's work?

Our Interaction with Family

Family may be the area of our lives that requires the most management. In addition to the everyday pressures of relating to one another as parents and children, there are societal pressures that pull at the fabric of family life.

The family, however, is here by God's design. In Gen. 3 we see that God placed Adam and Eve together as husband and wife. God blessed Adam and Eve and told them to be fruitful and increase in number. There are many Scriptures in both the Old and New Testament that give advice relating to one another as spouses, parents, and children. See Deut. 11:19–21; Matt. 19:14–15 for a couple examples.

It's important, then, that we manage our family obligations well. The family should be a place where children are loved, nurtured, protected, trained, and disciplined, where parents model love and mutual respect, and where God is honored. Following God's instructions for the family will lead to a fulfilled life. Always keep in mind, we are all part of a family on earth, and we have the privilege of being a part of God's family.

All aspects of our stewardship responsibility are important, but probably none is more important than the family. Someone has said that of all our possessions the only ones we will take with us into eternity are our children. We must keep in mind that our children are not clones of ourselves, but need to be encouraged to develop their unique personalities and the gifts that God has given them. They are not given to us to fulfill our dream, but to fulfill God's design and will for them. What an awesome responsibility and privilege!

Many people live in single parent families, blended families, and other variations brought about by life's circumstances. Others have chosen to remain single. But we are products of a family, and we are members of the family of God. God calls all of us to be good stewards of the life He has entrusted to us. That includes building healthy relationships with those who are related to us through human families.

Our Interaction with Family	
Model the Christian life at home	Deut. 11:19–21
Love your family	1 Cor. 13:4–8
Have healthy relationships with each other	Eph. 5:22–6:4

Bringing Glory to God

The aim of our lives is to glorify God, and we do that, in part, by being good stewards of all that He has given to us. That includes our relationships, our money, and our selves.

Life Is . . .	
Like a shadow	1 Chron. 29:15; Eccles. 6:12
Swifter than a weaver's shuttle	Job 7:6
A breath	Job 7:7
Swifter than a runner	Job 9:25
A mere handbreadth	Ps. 39:5
A mist that vanishes	James 4:14

The Apostle Paul said, "So whether you eat or drink or whatever you do, do it all for the glory of God" (1 Cor. 10:31). Someone has captured the heart of that Scripture in the popular question, "What Would Jesus Do?" Stewardship—managing our lives with God in mind—involves living every day to the glory of God. As we learn more about the Lord through His Word and His Holy Spirit, we will get better at making decisions that glorify Him and are a blessing for others: Each of us can be an influence in our culture, affecting others for good and bringing glory to our heavenly Father.

Our life here on earth is only a speck in time compared to eternity. When we choose to live for the Lord, we glorify God and He fulfills His promises in and through our lives. This is the abundant life promised in John 10:10, "I have come that they may have life, and have it to the full."

What might you have to change in order to be a good steward of the life God has given you?

To Learn More

Experiencing God: How to Live the Full Adventure of Knowing and Doing the Will of God by Henry T. Blackaby and Claude V. Kind

Having a Mary Heart in a Martha World by Joanna Weaver

In His Steps by Charles Sheldon

The Practice of the Presence of God by Brother Lawrence

Disciplines of a Beautiful Woman by Anne Ortlund

Reaching for the Invisible God by Philip Yancey

All additional books and resources are available from Wesleyan Publishing House at www.wesleyan.org/wph or by calling 800.4.WESLEY.

Personal Spiritual Journal

DATE _____

_____

_____

_____

_____

_____

_____

_____

_____

_____

_____

_____

_____

My Prayer Today—

_____

_____

_____

_____

CHAPTER 8

Becoming Part of the Family

Fellowship

> *From him the whole body, joined and held together by every*
> *supporting ligament, grows and builds itself up in love, as*
> *each part does its work.*
>
> —Ephesians 4:16

 **Bible Basics**

Ephesians 4:2–6, 11–16

²Be completely humble and gentle; be patient, bearing with one another in love. ³Make every effort to keep the unity of the Spirit through the bond of peace. ⁴There is one body and one Spirit—just as you were called to one hope when you were called— ⁵one Lord, one faith, one baptism; ⁶one God and Father of all, who is over all and through all and in all. . . . ¹¹It was he who gave some to be apostles, some to be prophets, some to be evangelists, and some to be pastors and teachers, ¹²to prepare God's people for the works of service, so that the body of Christ may be built up ¹³until we all reach unity in the faith and in the knowledge of the Son of God and become mature, attaining to the whole measure of the fullness of Christ. ¹⁴Then we will no longer be infants, tossed back and forth by the waves, and blown here and there by every wind of teaching and by the cunning and craftiness of men in their deceitful scheming. ¹⁵Instead, speaking the truth in love, we will in all things grow up

into him who is the Head, that is Christ. [16]From him the whole body, joined and held together by every supporting ligament, grows and builds itself up in love, as each part does its work.

 Connecting God's Word to Life

Where do you begin to see yourself contributing to the life of your church?

God's Team

Everyone loves to be on a team, especially a winning team. There is greater strength in a team than in any of its individual members. That strength is the power of shared goals and a common vision. It is the joy of working together to win. It is the relationships that develop through the ups and downs, the victories and setbacks of team life. There is a team dynamic, an X-factor, that develops within a team that cannot be easily explained but must be experienced to be understood.

The family of faith is a team. We function together more powerfully than any one of us could alone. There is a dynamic within the body of Christ that, like the X-factor of a winning team, must be experienced to be appreciated.

Let's take a look at some of the components that create this *fellowship* within the family of God. These items are a part of what makes a team of believers uniquely powerful together. Here's what it's like to be on God's team.

Baptism

Every team has its own rituals and traditions. Baseball teams are notoriously superstitious. Many baseball players, for instance, will avoid stepping on the chalk lines of the baseball diamond. Football teams have their own rituals, such as the coin toss at the start of the game and the pep talk at halftime. A team gains identity and solidarity from its traditions.

There are important traditions associated with the family of God as well. The most important of these are called *sacraments*. They are rituals that were instituted by Jesus in order to bring us closer to God. More powerful than mere human traditions, these sacred rites are actually a means of grace. When we participate in them, we communicate with God in a special way.

The first of these is *baptism*.

Jesus Himself was baptized with water (Matt. 3:13–16), and He commanded His disciples to baptize others as they went into the world with this gospel story (Matt. 28:16–20). His public ministry was launched with His baptism, and His final instructions to the disciples included the command to baptize. Why was this "dip in the brook" so important? Why would being baptized be important for me?

> There are important traditions associated with the family of God. More powerful than mere human traditions, these sacred rites are actually a means of grace.

Reasons to Be Baptized

Here are a few reasons why baptism has been significant to Christians from New Testament times until now.

It's a Public Statement of Faith

By this act, the person who is baptized declares to the world that he or she is a Christian. That's why baptism for new believers is often held out-of-doors in a public place. It is a clear way to announce that someone has joined the team! Even if baptism is held in church or a semi-private setting, the meaning is the same. It declares to all present that the individual has chosen to follow Christ.

It's a Statement of Accountability

At baptism, we are asked to declare our intention to live for Christ from then on. An affirmative response puts us "on the record" as being serious about following Christ. We make a statement to our teammates, our brothers and sisters in Christ, that we aim to live a new life.

It's a Symbol of Salvation

Baptism is a graphic reminder of what happened in us when we were saved. When we pledged our faith in Christ, His blood washed away our sins and made us a part of His family. It is as if the person that we used to be died, just as Christ died on the cross, and was raised to a new life. Baptism illustrates the cleansing of our lives by "washing with water." It also illustrates our death and resurrection with Christ (Rom. 6:1-4). Baptism does not wash away our sins—it merely illustrates that work of God in our hearts.

It's a Statement of Unity

Baptism is a time of celebration, like the victory lap after a race or a homecoming parade for an Olympic champion. It builds morale for a team to realize that others have joined the family of faith, taking a public stand for all to see.

Have you been baptized? List reasons why you would consider being baptized.

Ways to Be Baptized

The methods of baptism have been the object of strong discussion throughout the history of the church. There are three basic methods—often called *modes*—that may be used. Each one is valid.

Modes of Baptism	
Mode	**Description**
Immersion	The candidate for baptism is totally immersed in water. May be done outdoors in a river, lake, or other body of water, or indoors in a baptismal tank. Many prefer this mode because it graphically depicts our death and resurrection with Christ.
Pouring	Water is poured over the candidate's head, flowing down over much of the body. This is frequently used where access to open water is not available or is felt unnecessary. It provides a visual reminder that we have been washed by the blood of Christ.
Sprinkling	A small amount of water is sprinkled on the candidate's head. This mode is used for infant baptism and for those candidates who are physically unable to be baptized by immersion or pouring. Also, some churches simply prefer this mode. The sprinkling is symbolic of our cleansing by the blood of Christ.

Who Should Be Baptized

While there may be some disagreements concerning the preferred mode of baptism, there is unanimous agreement that all believers should be baptized. *Believer's baptism* is the term for the baptism of adults who have made a profession of faith in Christ.

Many churches also baptize infants. Why would we do that, since an infant cannot make a decision to accept Christ as Savior?

We may baptize infants because we believe that God's grace extends to all people who are not able to choose right from wrong. The Bible teaches that those who are too young to understand the truth are not responsible for the truth (see Mark 10:13–16; Acts 2:38–39). When a person reaches the "age of accountability"—in other words, an age when he or she is old enough to understand the difference between right and wrong and respond to the gospel—that person becomes accountable to God. Prior to that time, they are under the protection of God's grace. This is called the *prevenient grace* of God—the grace that "goes before." Parents may choose to have their infants baptized as an acknowledgement of God's grace and of their own faith in Christ.

Whether as an infant or as an adult, every believer should be baptized!

What questions do you have about baptism and whether or not you should be baptized?

Lord's Supper

The Lord's Supper. Communion. The Eucharist. Commemoration of the Last Supper. Breaking of Bread.

All of these terms refer to the same event in church life. When Christ was facing the last hours of His life before crucifixion, He instructed His disciples to prepare a special meal (see Matt. 26:26–29; Luke 22:14–10). At that meal, Jesus instituted the second sacrament of the Church, the Lord's Supper. Today, we continue to observe this ritual as reminder of Christ's death and a means of growing closer to God.

Old Testament Roots

Since the days when God miraculously delivered the Israelites from slavery in Egypt, Jewish people have observed the feast of Passover. This feast commemorates the crucial event that moved the Egyptian king to release the Hebrew people from slavery (see Exod. 11 and 12).

On that fateful night, the angel of death moved through the land killing the firstborn son in every home. But houses where blood was sprinkled on the doorposts were spared. These houses were "passed over." (See illustration on p. 39.)

On the night before He was crucified, Christ ate the Passover meal with His disciples. He told them of a new and far greater salvation that God was bringing to the world. This deliverance from captivity would no longer be remembered as "then and there" but would be experienced "here and now." He was speaking of His death, which brought deliverance from sin.

Passover: The Old Covenant	The Lord's Supper: The New Covenant
Commemorates deliverance from slavery in Egypt	Recalls our deliverance from sin
Applies only to Jewish people	Is for all who believe in Christ
Is a memory of past glory	Is a celebration of present reality

Remembering Christ's Death

When Christ talked with His disciples that night, He told them to remember this new arrangement, the *new covenant*, that God was making with them (see Luke 22:19). Paul the Apostle restated that instruction to the church at Corinth (see 1 Cor. 11:23–26). When we observe the Lord's Supper, we are following Jesus' command to remember the salvation that He provided for us. This act brings us into close fellowship, or *communion,* with God.

In his instructions about the Lord's Supper, Paul warned against receiving this sacrament in an "unworthy manner" and made it clear that the Lord's Supper is for members of the Lord's family only (see 1 Cor. 11:27–30). A person should be in a right standing with God when participating in the Lord's Supper.

Here are important points to remember about the Lord's Supper.

- It is a time to remember the death of Christ and to be thankful for the sacrifice He made.

- It is a time for self-examination and for seeking forgiveness for things in our lives that are displeasing to Him.

- It is to be observed periodically by Christians meeting together.

- It is for believers only, since those who do not know Christ have an incomplete understanding of the true meaning of the Lord's Supper.

Communion is a time for celebrating our unity as a team and remembering the sacrifice of our Lord.

Have you observed the Lord's Supper since you became a Christian? Describe your experience and how you felt as you joined in.

The Church

If you worked for a large corporation, you might have coworkers that lived in various parts of the country, even around the world. Although you had separate workplaces, you'd still have the same corporate goals and objectives. You'd be part of the same team.

The church of Jesus Christ is like that. There are millions of Christians who live in many countries around the world and worship in churches with different names, yet we all belong to Christ.

One Tree, Many Branches

For more than 1000 years after Christ lived here on earth, the church more or less functioned as a single unit. There were no denominations, as we now know them, and all who called themselves Christian were part of one church, whose earthly leader was located in Rome.

Over time, however, certain incorrect ideas became common, and various practices developed that were a concern to many people.

One of those concerned persons was a German monk named Martin Luther, who lived in the sixteenth century. In 1517, he posted a ninety-five-point document—his list of protests against the church—on a church door in the town of Wittenberg. He hoped to stir debate over a number of issues that troubled him. Initially, not much happened. Within a few months, however, reaction to Luther's document became quite strong. Over time, those who agreed with his protests came to be known as *Protestants*. Some formed churches separate from the Roman church.

In the next two hundred fifty years or so—until about 1800—many of the oldest denominations in the Protestant family came into being. Some were formed by reformers like Luther. Others were started by revivalists like John Wesley, the eighteenth-century English clergyman who started the Methodist movement. Since then, new Christian denominations have been formed occasionally by revival or reform movements.

Today, there are many denominations as Christians have gathered themselves into the groups that they believe best represent the teaching of Christ. All strive to faithfully follow the teachings of Jesus but operate independently of one another.

What do you think are the key beliefs that make a church part of the Christian family?

Teamwork

Every member of a team is responsible to the others. In the sport of hockey, for instance, teamwork is evident in every game. Veteran players set an example for the younger players. If a member of the opposing team roughs up the goaltender, the goalie's teammates come to his defense. When the coach gives instruction, the players all follow his direction whether they are rookies or veterans.

Team responsibilities exist in the family of faith just as they do in sports. We have lateral responsibilities—responsibilities to other members of our team—this is called *interdependence*. We have vertical responsibilities—responsibilities to those over us in the faith such as pastors—this is called *accountability*. We have downline responsibility for those who are younger in the faith—this is called *mentoring*. We have responsibility to all members of the family of faith to live our lives faithfully—this is *Christian citizenship*. At the apex of it all, we have responsibility to and will give an account to the Head Coach—Christ.

Relationship within the Body	Scripture
Interdependence	Gal. 6:1–2; Rom. 13:1
Accountability	Rom. 13:17
Mentoring	1 Kings 19:19–21; 2 Kings 2:1–18; Rom. 13:7
Christian Citizenship	Rom. 12:9–21
Ultimate Accountability	Rom. 14:12

Describe your relationship to other believers—for example, those at your local church, your pastor, Christians in other denominations.

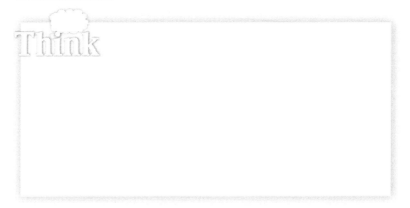

Joining the Team

As individuals, we like the idea of being in charge, being independent, and living by our own rules. As members of the body of Christ, however, we are accountable to God. We are dependent on Him for life itself and are interdependent with our brothers and sisters in the faith. We need one another for love, support, and understanding, and we submit ourselves to the authority of Christ. That's quite an adjustment! But in the family of God, what we give up is of lesser value than what we obtain. That's the value of the team.

We Need Each Other

Every Christian needs to be connected with a local unit of the body of Christ. While there have always been religious hermits, those locked away from the world in a vain attempt to keep sin at bay, the thundering call from 2000 years of Christian history is that we really do need each other (see Heb. 10:25).

Saint Paul wrote two letters—books we call them now—to a young church in the city of Corinth. In one of these letters, he spoke at length about the need for all believers to pool their various gifts and talents together so that the body of Christ might be healthy and growing. He likened the church to a human body, which has various parts, each necessary for the body to function properly (see 1 Cor. 12:12–31). The church needs us, and we need the church!

We must have interaction with the body of Christ to be strong and healthy believers. There are exceptional cases, individuals who thrived in spirit while cut off from the rest of the body of Christ due to imprisonment, extended illness, geographic isolation, or some other circumstance. God's grace was adequate in such extremes.

> No matter how gifted we may be, alone we have only the power of one. Joined with other believers in a healthy body, we greatly expand our impact for God and good.

But in our normal cycle of life, isolation breeds spiritual dwarfs with a very limited worldview and little or no opportunity to exercise their spiritual gifts for the common good. It is the wholesome interaction of relationships within the body that fosters maturity and allows for the exercise of gifts and talents. It helps create the strength that only comes from standing together.

Maximum Impact

Let's recall the example of a hockey team. One player, no matter how skilled, gifted, and determined, is no match for another team and can never win a game single-handedly. So it is with us. No matter how gifted we may be, alone we are just that—alone—and have only the power of one. Joined with other believers in a healthy body, we greatly expand our impact for God and good.

In the Old Testament book of Leviticus, we find this incredible truth, "Five of you will chase a hundred and a hundred of you will chase ten thousand, and the enemies will fall by the sword before you" (26:8).

Do the math. Five with God took on 100—a ratio of 1 to 20. One hundred with God took 10,000—a ratio of 1 to 100. The number of "good guys" went up from 5 to 100. The number of "bad guys" went up from 100 to 10,000 and still there was a promise of victory. Together we are stronger.

That's called synergy: maximized output resulting from working together. There is synergy in the body of Christ. Isolation fosters desolation; partnerships foster power. Independence fosters loneliness; togetherness fosters strength.

In what ways are you connecting in your church? Which Sunday School class or discipleship group have you joined?

The Church Universal and the Local Church

The Church—all true believers in Jesus Christ—is an awesome array of people from every point in history and every conceivable racial, geographic, cultural, and language group. That is known as the *Church Universal.* When assembled together, as the Bible promises will occur at the last days (see Rev. 7:9–17), the Church Universal will be an incredible gathering, the magnitude and scope of which we can only imagine. We, too, will be a part of that incredible gathering as we remain true to Christ as Savior. That grand assembly will be the Church in its most expansive and exciting reality.

The Church in our time has many valid expressions around the world. In other words, there is one true Church, yet there may be many *local churches.* Practices and customs may vary from one congregation to the next. Churches may exist under a variety of names. Positions on issues of lesser importance may differ. There are many ways of worshiping together, and some Christians will staunchly defend their way of "doing church." But that's like bickering with your brother or sister over who should have the TV remote control. We are still family, even when we feud over how that family will function.

The true Church is one, and we are all part of that family through faith in Jesus Christ. We have accepted Him as Savior. That's the basis of family living. We may disagree over the details of family life, but we all belong.

These various expressions of church life actually give us strength as a body.

Different approaches to these matters may appeal to different individuals. If all churches were exactly the same, how boring and limited we would be! Our different approaches to church life allow people to seek and find a church home that is an authentic part of the body of Christ yet is suited to their own needs.

Remember, though, that not all groups who use the word *church* to define themselves accept the clear teaching of the Bible on matters of salvation and other vital issues. When seeking fellowship with other believers, we must be careful to associate with those who are, in truth, members of the family of faith.

> When seeking fellowship with other believers, we must be careful to associate with those who are, in truth, members of the family of faith.

Finding a Local Church

After accepting Christ as Savior, one of the most crucial questions you must answer is this: where will I make my church home? This will be the place where you will invest your life for the kingdom, use your gifts in ministry, and receive teaching and encouragement in the faith. This is no small decision.

Christians sometimes select a local church based on good but secondary factors, such as:

- Proximity to home
- Association with family
- Appearance of facilities
- Quality of music
- Personality of the pastor

While these factors may initially attract you to a particular congregation, there are some other, more important issues you will want to consider. Here are some questions you might ask when considering association with a local church:

- Does this church accurately teach the truth of Scripture?
- Are people coming to Christ through the ministries of the church?
- Will I have a place of meaningful ministry in this church?
- Do I sense the presence of the Holy Spirit when I worship there?

- Do the sermons help me understand the faith and cope with everyday life?

- Do the people have a unified passion to build the Kingdom?

If the answers to these questions are all positive, then you might consider secondary factors such as the music, the facilities, and the church programs. If the answers to your first six questions were "yes," then it's likely that the secondary factors will be positive also.

Here are some other questions you might ask as you look for a local church:

- What is the church's statement of faith? Does it fit with what I know about the Bible?

- What are mission, vision, and core values of the church? Does the congregation seem to have a clear idea of why it exists and what it is doing?

- What is the congregation's position on important social issues such as abortion, homosexuality, pornography, and euthanasia?

- What am I looking for in a church? Why am I looking for these things— to serve others or to be served myself?

A healthy local church is the essence of the body of Christ. The Apostle Paul drew a parallel between the relationship that exists in a healthy marriage and the relationship that exists between Christ and the church. He said that Christ loves the church and gave His life for it (see Eph. 5:22–33). Jesus said that He would build the church and that even hell could not stop it! (Matt. 16:13–18).

So the church really is important. And as a new believer, you will need to become a part of it. Select a congregation carefully, commit to it fully, and participate in it gladly. There are no perfect churches, so seek fellowship in a church not perfection. You will discover the great joy of life in a healthy local church.

What are some of the preferences you have that affect your choice of a church? Which ones are negotiable? Which ones will you not compromise?

Joining a Church

Perhaps you have already found a healthy local church to call home. Since you have already decided to make this your church home, you have joined the group in one sense. Membership in the Church Universal is based only on your faith in Christ. When you accepted Him as your Savior, you "joined" the Church.

Yet you should consider formalizing your relationship with a local congregation by becoming a member of that church.

Why?

Let's return to the analogy of a sports team. When you join a team, you're given a uniform. You wear the colors of your team. That identifies you as one of the group, fosters loyalty to the team, and, as a practical matter, makes it easier to play the game.

When you join a local church, you become part of that local team. There are good reasons for doing that.

- It makes clear that you agree with that local church's mission and vision.

- It places you in an accountability relationship with that congregation.

- It lets the others know they can count on you for support.

- It may make you eligible for ministry or leadership responsibilities.

When you join a church, you come off the sidelines and into the game. You become a fully functioning member of the team. Being a part of a healthy local church is a great and worthwhile experience. Go ahead; put on the colors!

Privileges of Membership	Responsibilities of Membership
Fellowship with other believers	Support of others by prayer, presence, ministry, and finances
Input on direction and vision for future	Support of the church's mission
Protection and support of the Body	Promote the ministry of the church
Opportunities for leadership	Live a life that is a positive witness to the faith
Selection of pastoral leadership as needed	Serve in leadership roles as selected
"Wear the colors"—Be part of the team	"Wear the colors"—Be part of the team

Can a person be a Christian and not join a church? Why or why not?

 **To Learn More**

Common Ground edited by Everett Leadingham

Seize the Day by H. C. Wilson

We Hold These Truths by Earle Wilson

LifeKeys: Discovering . . . Who You Are, Why You're Here, What You Do Best by Sandra Krels Hirsh, Jane A. G. Kise, and David Stark

People Just Like Us by Norman G. Wilson

Who's ~~On~~ First edited by Everett Leadingham

All additional books and resources are available from Wesleyan Publishing House at www.wesleyan.org/wph or by calling 800.4.WESLEY.

Personal Spiritual Journal

DATE _____

_____

_____

_____

_____

_____

_____

_____

_____

_____

_____

_____

_____

_____

_____

_____

My Prayer Today—

_____

_____

_____

Scripture Index

Books of the Bible with Abbreviations

Old Testament

Genesis	Gen.
Exodus	Exod.
Leviticus	Lev.
Numbers	Num.
Deuteronomy	Deut.
Joshua	Josh.
Judges	Judg.
Ruth	Ruth
1 Samuel	1 Sam.
2 Samuel	2 Sam.
1 Kings	1 Kings
2 Kings	2 Kings
1 Chronicles	1 Chron.
2 Chronicles	2 Chron.
Ezra	Ezra
Nehemiah	Neh.
Esther	Esther
Job	Job
Psalms	Ps.
Proverbs	Prov.
Ecclesiastes	Eccles.
Song of Solomon	Song of Sol.
Isaiah	Isa.
Jeremiah	Jer.
Lamentations	Lam.
Ezekiel	Ezek.
Daniel	Dan.
Hosea	Hos.
Joel	Joel
Amos	Amos
Obadiah	Obad.
Jonah	Jon.
Micah	Mic.
Nahum	Nah.
Habbakuk	Hab.
Zephaniah	Zeph.
Haggai	Hag.
Zechariah	Zech.
Malachi	Mal.

New Testament

Matthew	Matt.
Mark	Mark
Luke	Luke
John	John
Acts	Acts
Romans	Rom.
1 Corinthians	1 Cor.
2 Corinthians	2 Cor.
Galatians	Gal.
Ephesians	Eph.
Philippians	Phil.
Colossians	Col.
1 Thessalonians	1 Thess.
2 Thessalonians	2 Thess.
1 Timothy	1 Tim.
2 Timothy	2 Tim.
Titus	Titus
Philemon	Philem.
Hebrews	Heb.
James	James
1 Peter	1 Pet.
2 Peter	2 Pet.
1 John	1 John
2 John	2 John
3 John	3 John
Jude	Jude
Revelation	Rev.

Personal Spiritual Journal

_____

_____

_____

_____

_____

_____

_____

_____

_____

_____

_____

_____

_____

_____

My Prayer Today—

_____

_____

_____

_____

Personal Spiritual Journal

DATE _____

_____

_____

_____

_____

_____

_____

_____

_____

_____

_____

_____

_____

_____

_____

_____

My Prayer Today—

_____

_____

_____

_____

Personal Spiritual Journal

DATE _____

_____

_____

_____

_____

_____

_____

_____

_____

_____

_____

_____

_____

_____

My Prayer Today—

_____

_____

_____

_____

Personal Spiritual Journal

DATE _____

_____

_____

_____

_____

_____

_____

_____

_____

_____

_____

_____

_____

_____

_____

My Prayer Today—

_____

_____

_____

_____

SPIRITUAL FORMATION

Do not conform any longer to the pattern of this world, but be transformed by the renewing of your mind. Then you will be able to test and approve what God's will is—his good, pleasing and perfect will.

SALVATION

Salvation is found in no one else, for there is no other name under heaven given to men by which we must be saved.

SCRIPTURE

All Scripture is God-breathed and is useful for teaching, rebuking, correcting and training in righteousness, so that the man of God may be thoroughly equipped for every good work.

EVANGELISM

"Come, follow me," Jesus said, "and I will make you fishers of men."

HOLINESS

It is God's will that you should be sanctified. . . .

WORSHIP

Let everything that has breath praise the Lord. Praise the Lord.

STEWARDSHIP

Love the Lord your God with all your heart and with all your soul and with all your mind and with all your strength. The second is this: love your neighbor as yourself. There is no commandment greater than these.

FELLOWSHIP

From him the whole body, joined and held together by every supporting ligament, grows and builds itself up in love, as each part does its work.

Acts 4:12

 *Knowing Christ: believing*

Romans 12:2

 *Knowing Christ: believing*

Matthew 4:19

 Knowing Christ: believing

2 Timothy 3:16–17

 Knowing Christ: believing

Psalm 150:6

 Knowing Christ: believing

1 Thessalonians 4:3

 Knowing Christ: believing

Ephesians 4:16

 Knowing Christ: believing

Mark 12:30–31

 Knowing Christ: believing